A Westminster Parliamentarian

Edited by David Hinchliffe MP

The fans' Media Petition: Ray Gent (centre - holding petition) presents it to David Hinchliffe MP and Lord Geoffrey Lofthouse outside the Houses of Parliament in March 2002. (Photo: Peter Lush)

LONDON LEAGUE PUBLICATIONS Ltd.

A Westminster XIII
Parliamentarians and Rugby League

© Copyright contributors. Foreword © Richard Caborn MP. Introduction ©David Hinchliffe M.P. The moral right of the contributors to be identified as the authors has been asserted.

Photographs may not be reproduced without permission. All photos copyright to the photographer.

Front cover photos: Top: Bradford Bulls versus St Helens 1997 Challenge Cup Final (Photo: David Williams); Bottom: Leeds versus Leigh 1971 Challenge Cup Final (Photo: Courtesy Robert Gate);

Back cover photos: Northern Ford Premiership 2001 Grand Final: Oldham versus Widnes (Peter Lush); David Hinchliffe MP (Photo: Courtesy David Hinchliffe MP)

This book is sold subject to the condition that it shall not, by way of trade or otherwise, be lent, resold, hired out or otherwise circulated without the publisher's prior consent in any form of binding or cover other than that in which it is published and without a similar condition including this condition being imposed on the subsequent purchaser.

A CIP catalogue record for this book is available from the British Library.

First published in Great Britain in October 2002 by:
London League Publications Ltd., P.O. Box 10441, London E14 0SB

ISBN: 1-903659-08-6 (hardback)
ISBN: 1-903659-09-4 (paperback)

Cover design by:	Stephen McCarthy Graphic Design
	46, Clarence Road London N15 5BB
Layout and design:	Peter Lush
Printed and bound by:	Bath Press Limited
	Lower Bristol Road, Bath BA2 3BL

Profits from the sale of this book will go to a fund administered by the All-Party Parliamentary Rugby League Group to support good causes within the game.

The chapters in this book do not necessarily represent the views of the All-Party Parliamentary Rugby League Group.

Foreword

I suspect that most outsiders, looking in on Westminster, would probably be surprised to learn just how many of my political colleagues have a deep and genuine interest in sport.

This book demonstrates the commitment and passion of a number of MPs and peers for the great sport of Rugby League. Its chapters offer a unique insight into what the game means to them personally, into their knowledge and experience of the 13-a-side game.

I grew up in a soccer city but have been a keen follower of Rugby League since the advent of the Sheffield Eagles. Being present at Wembley for their great victory over Wigan in 1998 is one of the finest sporting memories of my life.

It was also a particular privilege to be asked to present the Challenge Cup trophy at this year's Murrayfield final between Wigan and St Helens. The Rugby League final never fails to offer the best of entertainment and it is always a pleasure to be amongst the colourful and good-humoured crowds from our Rugby League communities.

The All-Party Parliamentary Rugby League Group has been a vigorous and effective lobby for the sport at Westminster since its formation in 1988. Its members deserve great credit for their part in fighting the undoubted prejudice against the game that has existed in some quarters for many years. They have played a crucially important role in the lifting of barriers that have in the past prevented the game's expansion.

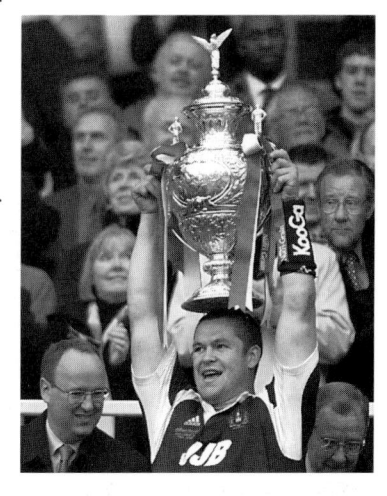

I am certain you will enjoy reading this excellent book, which is a fitting celebration of the Group's forthcoming fifteenth birthday.

Rt Hon Richard Caborn MP, Minister for Sport

Photo: Andy Farrell, having just been presented with the Challenge Cup at the 2002 Final by Richard Caborn MP (Photo: David Williams)

Introduction

The All-Party Parliamentary Rugby League Group reaches its fifteenth anniversary early in 2003. The publication of this collection of articles by several of our members seemed an appropriate way to celebrate its work while also raising some money for good causes within the game.

There is the potential for a pretty obscure pub quiz question about the origins of our Group: how many would know of the connection between the death of a famous British monarch and a Rugby League birth? The answer is that the idea for the Group arose from discussions in the very room in which Oliver Cromwell and his fellow parliamentarians reputedly signed the death warrant of King Charles I in 1649.

Following the 1987 general election, the handful of genuine Rugby League enthusiasts in the Commons at the time – such as Geoff Lofthouse, Kevin McNamara, Merlyn Rees, Doug Hoyle, Laurie Cunliffe, the late Roger Stott, and Lords Jack Brookes and David Swinton – were joined by a number of other younger MPs, whose main sporting passion was the 13-a-side code.

Prominent among them was the Makerfield Labour MP, Ian McCartney, who was allocated as an office one of the four desks in the 'King Charles room', an annex to the Cloisters, next to Westminster Hall, deep in the bowels of the Commons. As a fellow new boy, I was given a desk in the corridor immediately adjacent to the room, alongside fellow Rugby League supporter Alice Mahon, the MP for Halifax.

The formation of an all-party group – envisaged as a voice for our great game in Parliament – was McCartney's idea and in next to no time we had around 80 MPs and peers signed up for the cause.

Relations with Rugby Union – still theoretically 'amateur' at that stage – were a key agenda item. Group members had long recognised that Union's ban on even amateur Rugby League players changing codes severely limited League's ability to expand the code beyond its traditional boundaries. We had concrete proof that a number of top Rugby Union players were receiving generous rewards for playing and it was clear that Union's 'amateurism' rules were aimed more at outlawing Rugby League than professionalism.

Armed forces

We knew that Rugby Union's international expansion had come via British armed forces, which did not then permit the playing of League. Our meetings with the Ministry of Defence and hierarchy of the armed forces left us with the distinct impression that Rugby League was viewed in a similar light to something rather unpleasant stuck to a shoe. But through constant pressure, parliamentary questions and debates, as well as a sympathetic Sports Minister in Ian Sproat, by 1994 Rugby League was on the list of approved sports and being played in the Army, Navy and RAF. Forces teams would soon be entering the Rugby League Challenge Cup.

Bearing in mind the battle we had to obtain recognition, I was interested only recently to see the comments of Lt General Scott C. Grant that "Rugby League is the only sport played in the British Army which epitomises all of the qualities required by a soldier". He referred to "courage, determination, fitness, team-work, skill and – perhaps most importantly – discipline".

Parliament offers many opportunities to highlight a grievance and the group chose to exploit a range of procedural tactics in pressing League's cause. We moved amendments to the National Lottery Bill, aimed at blocking funding to those sports which discriminated against particular participants. Following contacts with Inland Revenue officials, we learned that their investigations had established that, at top level, Rugby Union was at least as professional as Rugby League. We subsequently upped our guerrilla tactics with my Sports (Discrimination) Bill, proposing to make it illegal for one sport to discriminate against those playing another.

The Group's efforts persuaded others to take notice of League's treatment by Union. The National Heritage Select Committee undertook an inquiry in early 1995, which found the attitude of Rugby Union to Rugby League both discriminatory and indefensible, proposing a block on public funding to Union until amended its rules. Later the same year, Rugby Union was forced by both internal and external pressure to finally abandon its long discredited 'amateurism' principle.

The All-Party Group played an important part in challenging Rugby Union's sporting apartheid and with the remarkable development of the Total RL.Com Conference, with teams now playing League in new territory right across England, we see the results. Freed from the nonsense of bans and proscriptions, sports men and women can play the sport of their choice.

For the most part, our group has had a positive relationship with those running Rugby League, but we have on a number of issues felt it necessary to take a fundamentally different position to that formally adopted by the game. With the advent of Super League in 1995, we voiced in Parliament the fans' concern about proposals to merge such famous teams as Warrington and Widnes, and Featherstone Rovers, Castleford and Wakefield Trinity. The powers that be eventually backed off. But the experience underlined the need for a much more active supporter role within the game, which is why our Group has taken a very close interest in the development of Supporters Direct.

I suspect that some of the game's leading figures were also less than pleased when, led by Lord Geoffrey Lofthouse in the Lords, the group persuaded the Government to add the Rugby League Challenge Cup Final to the list of national sporting events which had to be retained for broadcasting on terrestrial TV.

Prejudice against League

While the changes in Union in 1995 have led to genuine improvements in relations between the codes, we still see far too many examples of prejudice against Rugby League. With our colleagues in the European Parliament's Inter Group for Rugby League – led by MEPs Brian Simpson and Terry Wynn – we have supported Treize Actif in its campaign for compensation for French Rugby League following the disastrous consequences of the Union inspired ban on the sport under the wartime Vichy regime. The recent publication of the report of the French Sport Minister's Commission of Inquiry into this disgraceful affair fully justifies longstanding League concerns and, along with our European colleagues, the Parliamentary Group will be pressing for action by the French Government.

The Group continues to campaign for the inclusion of Rugby League in such events as the Commonwealth Games. When asked why only Rugby Union was included in the 2002 Manchester games, the official response was that 'League did not play Sevens'. Bradford Bulls countered this argument in fine style a couple of weeks later when, having played St Helens in Super League on the previous evening and travelled overnight to London, they trounced Wasps to win the Middlesex Rugby Union Sevens at Twickenham.

Various commentators subsequently noted that the Middlesex Sevens appeared to get less coverage than normal in the London-based Sunday papers the following day, fuelling a longstanding concern of our group that Rugby League gets a far from fair crack of the whip from the media.

Frankly, we have lost track of the letters sent to the broadcasting media and individual newspapers over complaints we receive from supporters about either inaccurate or unfair reporting or grossly inadequate or non-existent coverage of the sport. At our last meeting before the 2002 summer recess, the group received a complaint from a woman supporter in Cornwall about a piece in a regional newspaper referring to Great Britain's heavy defeat in Australia in July. It read: 'It's a little too much to expect that we will be world beaters in a sport played only by whippet breeding northerners in between breaks down t' mine,' and typifies the attitudes which still prevail nearly a quarter of a century on from Eddie Waring.

As my colleague Andy Burnham points out in his chapter, soccer is now the official game of the media set. Rugby Union comes a close second in many of the broadsheets with League frequently nowhere to be seen. Union's club attendances have risen significantly in recent times. One wonders what the impact would be on the number of spectators at Rugby League matches if League's media coverage reached anywhere near the space accorded to Union and reflected the amount of genuine interest in the game way beyond its traditional areas.

And why, supporters ask the Group, should BBC 2's *Rugby* (Union) *Special* be broadcast nationwide while the *Super League Show* on the same channel is confined to just the north of England. As I write this introduction, I recall that yesterday morning's Radio 4 *Today* programme featured Leeds Tykes Rugby Union team's match, but made no mention of the Leeds Rhinos Rugby League game at which almost three times the number of spectators were present. My 'quality' Sunday broadsheet gives me as usual more than two full pages of Rugby Union and only a couple of obscure paragraphs of Rugby League which prove extremely difficult to find.

The petition

It was concerns such as these which led St Helens fan, Ray Gent, to organise a 30,000+ supporters' petition about media coverage which the Group presented to Parliament earlier this year. This issue - underpinned by a London based media's ignorance of our sport - is clearly unfinished business for our Group. We are determined to address a problem which undoubtedly holds back the progress of Rugby League as a major spectator sport.

As the following chapters show, there are few sports which can compete with Rugby League in terms of action, excitement, skill and importance to the communities in which they are played. My colleagues have encapsulated just a little of what makes Rugby League so special to its thousands of followers.

I would like to thank all the MPs and Peers who have contributed to this book. It is also appropriate to thank those supporters who have contributed to its financial success by becoming patrons. Finally, can I in particular thank our publishers, London League Publications Ltd. They proposed this project and I hope the end result will prove an interesting and enjoyable read.

David Hinchliffe MP
Secretary of the All-Party Rugby League Parliamentary Group

About the authors

Rt Hon Richard Caborn has been MP for Sheffield Central since 1983 and prior to that was a Member of the European Parliament. He has held a number of ministerial offices and is currently Minister for Sport.

Lord Jack Ashley was made a Life Peer in 1987 and previously was MP for Stoke on Trent South. He is a leading campaigner for people with sensory disabilities and is President of the RNID. He is President of Widnes Vikings RLFC.

Harold Best has been Member of Parliament for Leeds North West since 1997 and previously served as a West Yorkshire County Councillor. He serves on the Accommodation and Works and Environmental Audit Select Committees.

Andy Burnham has been Member of Parliament for Leigh since 2001. He previously worked for Tessa Jowell MP as a researcher and was a special advisor to Chris Smith as Secretary of State for Culture Media and Sport. He is a member of the Commons Health Select Committee.

James Clappison has been a Conservative Member of Parliament since 1992, representing Hertsmere. He was Parliamentary Private Secretary to Baroness Blatch from 1994 to 1995, and from 1995 to 1997 was Parliamentary Under-Secretary of State for the Environment.

Yvette Cooper has been Member of Parliament for Pontefract & Castleford since 1997. Prior to becoming an MP, she was a policy adviser to the Labour Treasury team and worked for *The Independent* newspaper from 1995 to 1997. She was a member of the Education and Employment Select Committee from 1997 to 1999, and is now Parliamentary Secretary at the Lord Chancellor's Department.

Tony Cunningham was elected as the Labour Member of Parliament for Workington in 2001. A former Member of the European Parliament, he is a qualified Rugby League and Rugby Union referee.

Rt Hon Frank Dobson has been MP for Holborn and St Pancras since 1979. He is a former Secretary of State for Health, and held various shadow cabinet posts for Labour while in opposition.

David Hinchliffe has been Labour Member of Parliament for Wakefield since 1987. Previously a Shadow Health Minister, he has been Chairman of the Commons Health Select Committee since 1997. He was the author of *Rugby's Class War* (London League Publications 2000).

Lord Doug Hoyle was made a Life Peer in 1997 and prior to that was Member of Parliament for Warrington North. He is a former Chairman of the Parliamentary Labour Party and currently Chairman of Warrington Wolves RLFC.

Lindsay Hoyle has been Member of Parliament for Chorley since 1997. The son of Lord Doug Hoyle, he is a former Chairman of Chorley RLFC. Before becoming the town's Labour MP, he was a Councillor in Chorley.

Peter Kilfoyle has been Labour MP for Liverpool Walton since 1991. He is a former Parliamentary Under-Secretary of State for Defence, and has also held government office in the Cabinet Office.

Lord Geoffrey Lofthouse was made a Life Peer in 1997 and previously represented Pontefract and Castleford in Parliament for the Labour Party. He is a former Deputy Speaker of the House of Commons and is President of the British Amateur Rugby League Association.

Rt Hon Ian McCartney has been Labour MP for Makerfield since 1987. He has held a number of ministerial positions and is currently Minister of State in the Department for Work and Pensions.

Rt Hon Kevin MacNamara has been MP for Kingston upon Hull North since 1966. He is a former Labour Spokesman on Northern Ireland, and held various shadow cabinet posts for Labour while in opposition.

Alice Mahon has been Labour MP for Halifax since 1987. She represents the UK on the North Atlantic Assembly. She was Parliamentary Private Secretary to Chris Smith MP in 1997 when he was Culture, Media and Sport Secretary.

Rt Hon Dr Sir Brian Mawhinney has been an MP since 1979 and now represents Cambridgeshire North West. He held a number of ministerial positions for the Conservatives, including Secretary of State for Transport, Minister of State for Northern Ireland, Minister of Health and Party Chairman.

Lord Peter Smith of Leigh was made a Life Peer in 1999. He is currently the Leader of Wigan Metropolitan Council, where he has been a Labour Councillor since 1978 and leader since 1991.

Derek Twigg has been Labour MP for Halton since 1997. He is currently a Government Whip, and was formerly a Parliamentary Private Secretary in the Department of Trade and Industry.

Derek Wyatt has been Labour MP for Sittingbourne and Sheppey since 1997. He is a former England RU international and serves on the Commons Culture Media and Sport Committee. He has written widely on Rugby Union. His last book was *Rugby DisUnion*; he is currently writing its sequel.

Patrons

We would like to thank the following for supporting the book as patrons.

Bill Anderson
Bradford Bulls
Bob Brown
Tony Chambers (Chair, Widnes Vikings RLFC)
Roy Close
Ken Davy
Alan Domville
Peter Elliott
John & Kath Etty
Phil Fearnley
Trevor Foster MBE
Peter Fox
Ray French
Len Garbett
Harold Genders
Mike Greetham
Martin Harrison
Peter Hirst
Huddersfield RL Club Players Assn
Brian Hughes
David Hughes (Chairman, London Broncos RFC)
Colin Hutton
Ian Jackson
Anthony Jenkins
Harry Jepson OBE

Bill Kilgallon OBE
Stuart Leadley
Richard Lewis (RFL Executive Chairman)
Richard D Lewis
Beverly Maderson
Derek Millis
Dr Stephen Morris
Bill Nelson
John Noon
Maurice Oldroyd (Chairman, BARLA)
David Oxley CBE
Nigel Riley
Bev Risman
Kevin Rudd (Scotland Students RL)
Ian Seabridge
Alex Service
Komal Shires
Councillor Kevin Swift
Eric Timmins
Michael & Sylvia Waite
Wakefield Trinity Wildcats RLFC
Nigel Waters
Nicholas Wheat
Dr Jack Whittaker
Graham Williams
Gerry Wright

Thank You

We would like to thank: David Williams, Peter Lush and Ken Coton for providing photos for the book; Robert Gate for providing historic photos, and for his advice on historic issues; Republic Media and Sportsbeat for providing photos of the Matchbox Rugby League championship; Stephen McCarthy, Michael O'Hare, Dave Farrar, Julia Hinchliffe and Stuart Alexander (Bath Press Ltd) for work on producing the book; and John Huxley from the RFL for help in publicising the book. The shirts at the start of each chapter were designed by Stephen McCarthy.

Derek Twigg MP is very grateful for the co-operation and help received from Tony Chambers, Neil Kelly and Andrew Kirchin from Widnes Vikings RLFC. Also the help from the *Widnes Weekly News* was invaluable.

Contents

		Page
1.	Lord Jack Ashley: A Chemic remembers	1
2.	Harold Best MP: The best type of Rugby	7
3.	Andy Burnham MP: Next door but one to Mick Martyn	11
4.	James Clappison MP: A Robin and a Rhino	15
5.	Yvette Cooper MP: Coming to terms with Tiger Town	19
6.	Tony Cunningham MP: Workington Town at Old Trafford	23
7.	Frank Dobson MP: A Clarence Street boy	29
8.	David Hinchliffe MP: It was nothing to do with a missed conversion	37
9.	Lord Doug Hoyle: Wolves by a whisker	45
10.	Lindsay Hoyle MP: Being Chorley's Chair	51
11.	Peter Kilfoyle MP: I'm sure I recognise that prop	57
12.	Lord Geoffrey Lofthouse: Not just a sport - a way of life	61
13.	Alice Mahon MP: Fax and figures	69
14.	Sir Brian Mawhinney MP: Taking comfort from the game	73
15.	Ian McCartney MP: Murrayfield to Murrayfield via Central Park, Wigan	75
16.	Kevin McNamara MP: Two shares in Hull Kingston Rovers	83
17.	Lord Peter Smith: Murphy's magic day	87
18.	Derek Twigg MP: Going back where they belong	95
19.	Derek Wyatt MP: Union and League merge - shock: horror	105

Rugby League Conference Lionhearts versus Featherstone Lions in the Challenge Cup December 2001, at Hemel Hempstead. The Conference has played a key role in developing the game in new areas. (Photo: Peter Lush)

Match Box Rugby League

In July 2002 several teams of MPs and Peers, along with the London Broncos played a Matchbox Rugby League competition. The event was organised by the London Broncos and the All-Party Parliamentary Rugby League Group, and raised money for Sport Relief.
Top: The Lancashire MPs team; bottom: The London Broncos.
(Photos: Sportsbeat, courtesy Republic Media)

Lord Jack Ashley: A Chemic remembers

Few people know the real words of the song commonly known as *John Brown's Body Lies a Mouldering in the Grave*. Far from being about this man's body, or his soul going marching on, the original words, which I learned as a child in Rugby League mad Widnes, were about their famous team.

"When Widnes go to Wembley to win the Rugby Cup,
When Widnes go to Wembley to win the Rugby Cup,
When Widnes go to Wembley to win the Rugby Cup,
They'll bring the Cup back home.
Glory, Glory Hallelujah.......they'll bring the Cup back home."

My amazement, when I was a little older, to find that the real Widnes words had been replaced by a parody about someone's body, knew no bounds. But it never dented my devoted enthusiasm for the town and its team - an emotion that has survived more than 70 years.

Not only did I know of the team's heroic exploits, I had actually shaken hands with its legendary captain, Paddy Douglas, who led the team at its first Wembley final in 1930. He was related to our next-door neighbour and paid occasional visits. Possibly a visit from the King might have created the same sense of excitement, but I doubt it.

So, because the next best thing from imbibing Rugby League with mother's milk, is to absorb it from the environment and atmosphere, I can claim to be a lifelong fan. But the club was in existence long before I was born in 1922. In 1895, together with 21 other, typically working class, north England clubs, Widnes became a founder member of the breakaway Northern Union after it split from the Rugby Football Union.

As the club developed, so did some of the players who became stars. Before the First World War the names of Billy Reid, Harry Taylor, the two O'Garra brothers and "Chick" Johnson became household names. Johnson was the club's first Great Britain international and his famous dribbled try in the 1914 "Rorke's Drift" deciding third test match against Australia in Sydney assured his place in the game's history. According to Tom Fleet, who compiled a detailed history of the Widnes club, historians still describe this as the most famous match in test history between Great Britain and Australia. In view of the many dramatic encounters since then, it certainly must have been some match.

Like many northern towns, Widnes was dominated by heavy industry. As the players worked mainly in the local ICI chemical factories the club's nickname became, to no one's surprise, "the Chemics". The team's activities were one of the most important means of entertainment, all the more so in the 1930s and 1940s because there was no television. During the periodic slumps, men - rarely women - turned to Rugby League as their main hobby and passion. The fortunes of the team practically determined the town's mood for the week.

Rugby League has never enjoyed the riches of today's football clubs and in the early days the clubs were mainly poor. Periodic financial difficulties were part of their history from the start. Massive transfer fees were unknown and no doubt the more impecunious teams were unable to pay any at all.

Widnes made a virtue of this necessity and periodically one of its proudest boasts, when the team was doing well, was that all 13 players were born locally. "Home grown local lads" was the defiant battle cry. The stars, heroes in a community of some 30,000, were big fish in a small pool. To wide-eyed youngsters like myself, they were gods.

It cost nothing to adore those gods. Designer shirts, shorts and boots hadn't been thought of and tattered jerseys, with worn shoes, was the uniform of many of us. In that environment, this attire was perfectly acceptable. The cost of admission to the boys enclosure was charitably derisory.

Wembley 1930

Although I was only eight-years-old when Widnes reached the Challenge Cup Final at Wembley in 1930, I have vivid memories of the football giants in their black and white striped jersey holding the huge, magical Cup aloft as the charabanc wended slowly through large crowds of cheering people.

Widnes had fielded 12 locally born players and only one from outside, a relatively old South African, Van Rooyen. At their next Wembley final in 1934, the team consisted entirely of Widnes born men. This was a powerful factor in creating spectator loyalty to their very own team.

Much later, as the game became more commercial, outside stars were drafted in. Notable among them were the legendary Jonathan Davies who came from Welsh Rugby Union and Martin Offiah, another Union signing, who became the fastest man in Rugby League. They increased the number of spectators who came to watch the team with its great variety of talents.

The journalists then were just as enterprising as today's tabloid writers. Vivid reports of the team's exploits and individual brilliance appeared regularly in the local press, thus feeding our omnivorous appetite for

Widnes 1933-4: Back: Robinson, Stevens, Chatterton, Hoey, Silcock, Ratcliffe, Millington. Front: Owens, Bradley, Stephens, McCue, Shannon, Jacks.
(Photo: Courtesy Robert Gate)

information. Gossip, speculation and dogmatic assertions were the order of the day. We just knew that "When Widnes got to Wembley" they would bring the Cup back home. If by some outrageous quirk of fortune they failed to do so, we had a ready excuse - it must have been the referee! No matter how brilliant your team, how can you win with a crooked referee? Occasionally, the wrath of spectators settled on unfortunate players. On one occasion after Widnes had lost at Wembley, and a winger had failed to hold a crucial scoring pass, some of us were talking to the father of one of my friends who had actually been at Wembley - one of the few "wealthy" families we knew. What happened with that winger, we asked. "Ah, he was dead drunk" came the reply. The idea that a drunken player would be allowed on the hallowed Wembley turf, or any other for that matter, was bizarre. But that outright condemnation brooked no argument. Even at that early age, I noted the unfairness of rugby spectators - and I can still remember the unfortunate winger's blackened name. Much later, a trusted friend of mine, who knew the player very well, said he was extremely abstemious. So much for the search for gossip - and scapegoats.

One of Widnes's great stars of the 1930s who also played for the national team, was Tommy McCue, a half-back. I was always perplexed that our opponents could not prevent an obvious trick for which McCue, and the other half-back, Tommy Shannon, were famous. It was the reverse pass.

Near the opponents' line, McCue would retrieve the ball from the scrum and dart to the left heading diagonally for the line. Shannon would run across behind him to McCue's right and while the opponents were trying to tackle McCue, he would slip a reverse pass to Shannon who came hurtling in to score.

This reverse pass became very famous throughout the Rugby League world, yet I could never understand why the opponents didn't all wait to demolish Shannon. I could never work it out. Possibly, if they did that too often, McCue would use Shannon as a diversion and score himself, or pass to a winger. But that was less dazzlingly successful than the reverse pass. This magical trick on the field became part of the folklore of the town and the delight of it youngsters.

Another outstanding player in the 1930s, Jimmy Hoey, secured his place in local and national history by becoming the first player in Rugby League to play and score in every match for his club in one season. He did this in 1932-33 with 83 goals and 21 tries in 40 games. However, Widnesians at the time though were kept in suspense because the last match was at Barrow and when the score, a defeat by 19-9 came through with Widnes scoring three tries but no goals, it was assumed Hoey had failed at the last hurdle. In fact, he had scored all three tries.

We had our share of brawny forwards who were hardly prolific scorers. One fixture in the team, a plodding hooker who was successful in the scrums, had never scored a try. One day, the miracle happened and he scored. The delighted bulldozer demanded that a photo be taken of the spot where he crossed the line. "Just so that everyone remembers it" he said.

Such stories were told and retold over the years by Widnesians who were devoted to their team. If it wasn't a fanatical following - and the people are too level-headed to be fanatical - it was a very enthusiastic one. Recalling great personalities, and great days, was one of the town's favourite pastimes.

So steeped in the team's exploits and traditions were the supporters that they accumulated impressively detailed knowledge of the team's history. Typical of many of them is Ken Merrifield, an old workmate of mine. We worked together as labourers on the furnaces of a copper smelting factory and both of us later became crane drivers. His perceptive comments at a Widnes rugby match were so good as to put the average coach to shame. He knew all the techniques and manoeuvres. When I spoke to him recently, he was able to name every single Widnes player in the 1930 Challenge Cup Final. His attitude and experience, like many Widnes supporters, explains why the team is part of the fabric and folklore of the town and commands such a dedicated group of followers.

Like all teams, Widnes has had its periods of success and failure but the highlights of its best times were a source of great pride. After a somewhat barren period, the club was elated at winning the Challenge Cup Final at

Wembley in 1964, though this was followed by more dismal years. In 1969, the club went 10 games without a single win. But in the 1970s, Widnes spirits were revived with the appointment of the great Vince Karalius as coach. A talented and tough forward, he played for St. Helens for some years and in his international hey day he was known as "the Wild Bull of the Pampas". The return of this local man as coach delighted the supporters and in 1975 Widnes were back at Wembley where they beat Warrington.

Two other Widnesians were, like Vince Karalius, outstanding players and coaches. Doug Laughton embellished the game and with him at the helm the club won every major honour from 1978-91. Frank Myler, a powerful and elusive halfback, made a major contribution to the team as a player and, as a coach he led Widnes to its first ever Division One Championship.

However, for all its fine traditions, the club was to suffer a crushing and humiliating blow when Super League was introduced. They failed to qualify for the competition and were consigned to the lower Premiership Division. Their separation from the top teams was inevitably damaging in every way. But in 2001 they won the Premiership Grand Final and were promoted to the Super League for the following season. Since then, they have established an unchallengeable claim to belong to Super League. Many commentators have said that the team has stunned the other Super League clubs by their vigorous and successful play. It is a great accomplishment to move upward from the lower division, but then to get among the leaders of Super League is well beyond expectation. Under the chairmanship of Tony Chambers, and the coaching of Neil Kelly, the Club's future in Rugby League is likely to be as glittering as the best times of its past.

Left: Lewis Jones - Leeds and Great Britain legend, remembered by Harold Best MP and Frank Dobson MP
(Photo: Courtesy Robert Gate)

Below: Oldham versus Leigh in the Northern Ford Premiership, February 2001.
(Photo: Peter Lush)

Harold Best MP:
2 The best type of Rugby

I first heard of 'rugby' when I was playing football with other boys during school playtime, A passing adult called out "you lads should be playing rugby".

I hadn't a clue what rugby was but guessed it to be a game like football. Later in my primary school years not long after the end of the Second World War, perhaps 1946, our teacher, Mr Ambler, who was followed by a Mr Cogan, (funny how some names stick) announced that we were going to Meanwood Park today and we were going to play rugby, because our school was a rugby school.

That afternoon, off we went in pairs on the 15 minute walk to the local park. We didn't have a sports field even though our school was considered a modern building. On arrival a rugby ball was produced and, to my surprise, some of the boys present knew what it was and how rugby was played (their claim). The teacher then said: "In this game the aim is simple, there are two sides and he split our group into even numbers of something like 18. He then said that we should remember who was on our side for later.

He explained that the idea was to carry the ball across a line marked by two jackets and place it on the ground. This was known as a try. He went on to say that whichever side had the ball could pass it to each other, but that we must not pass the ball forward. The opposing side should try and prevent a try being scored by tackling the boy with the ball.

We were then shown how to pass the ball and tackle by the handful of boys who already knew something of the game, supervised by the teacher,

After this explanation and coaching we then played a short game which was, to say the least, a right mix-up of roles by all concerned. After about 20 minutes of this we walked back to school, mud on our short trousers and jackets, or jumpers and our shoes covered in mud. Some two years later the school acquired some rugby shorts and jerseys, then our parents bought rugby boots, a huge expense at the time, certainly for my mam and dad, who spent many weeks deciding if they could afford rugby boots for me and if they could, should they buy them a least a size too big so that they would last for a year or two.

Anyway, we, Bentley Lane School, were on our way in this rugby game which I now knew to be Rugby League, which I was advised by my dad was different to Rugby Union and a much better game. My dad didn't exactly encourage me although he did tell me of some of his exploits when playing Rugby League for his school, For example, how he had carried two or three opponents on his back over the try line. I thought that if he were playing today someone would have got him round the legs, which is what we did to stop anyone. Even the biggest players couldn't run with you hanging onto their ankles.

The school team progressed and we were lucky enough to have the right mix of players, large and small (which is important in school rugby). I played in the forwards as a prop. I was big for my age and good at those things that seemed to matter: catching, passing and tackling. The team was a team in the best sense of the word, we had known each other since nursery school - we called it infants' school then. Thinking back, we had the benefit of playing together for years, not only at rugby, but as children and we knew each others' skills well.

My team played well enough to win the league we played in, beating our nearest rivals Buslingthorpe Lane School. They were known as "Buz" and they had their own pitch to play on. I learned later that this pitch was used by an open age amateur side and had been recovered from its days as a quarry by tipping domestic rubbish - mostly ash - from the coal fires in most people's homes then.

Rugby League was, I discovered, a game that could be played by men for money and I went to see such a match at Headingley, paid 6d (sixpence) to enter the boy's enclosure and I was amazed by the size of the crowd. Leeds were playing Hunslet in the Lazenby Cup and it was an amazing experience for me. There was no mistaking whose side the various supporters were on. I also learned that our teacher's insistence on playing by the rules was not always followed by these professionals and the crowd seemed to regard this as part of the entertainment.

Hunslet Schoolboys

Anyway, the next season as a 10-year-old, I was sent for "trials", (and I had no idea what the term trials meant) with others from my school: Tom Pollard and Fred Anderson as I remember it. We ended up being selected to play for Leeds Schools under-11s to play other sides of equal stature. My first game for Leeds City Schoolboys was against Hunslet Schoolboys at Parkside - a ground well-known by older Rugby League fans for its partisan crowd and being schoolboys didn't seem to make much of a difference. Looking back on this experience I suppose the crowd of some 200 or so paid us the compliment of taking our team seriously. We won, although I can't remember the score. It was a close game and I managed to cross the line in one of those series of forward movements that the rules permitted at the time. We were making perhaps five yards with every tackle and keeping the ball tight and it was my five yards that carried the ball over the Hunslet line.

My memory is not what it used to be and I could be mistaken about this but 1 remember Parkside having something like a dog track around it. I remember a woman running across it towards me, shouting at me for tackling her son in a manner which obviously did not please her. The referee was happy with the tackle, the touch-judge was happy with the tackle and neither the lad himself nor any of his team-mates thought anything was wrong with the tackle. It was one of those learning experiences which have been useful throughout my life - the lesson being "It doesn't matter what the facts are I have made up my mind". I have also learnt that prejudices formed when young, from older people, get passed on generation after generation. I accept that there is a place for passion and group loyalty, but it can get out of proportion, even in our great game of Rugby League.

I did play against Hunslet Schoolboys again, but this time in the over-11s and under-15s. This period of my schoolboy rugby was a joy for me and the others I played with. It's when we received some real training advice from a Mr Shepherd (I think) for us forwards - simple stuff which he expected us to carry out: never miss a tackle; never drop a pass; and be with the ball at all times, even if some fool on our side has kicked it up field.

It really was fun and exciting and each week I couldn't wait for Saturday's match to come around. My school then had a good team and we did very well in the league in which we played. There was real competition between the various towns and their school teams with one of the closest matches being against Hull City Schoolboys at The Boulevard. For this game I was left on the bench, but I still enjoyed being there in the intense atmosphere even for the school boy curtain raiser to the professional match. The easiest game was against Doncaster Schoolboys whose schools had just turned to Rugby League. A good memory from the first game I played against Doncaster was the sight of Lewis Jones sitting on the bench waiting to play for Leeds with whom he had just signed for the then record fee of £6,000.

The other games were good. My final game for Leeds City Schoolboys took place on a day I was to attend a job interview. My headmaster telephoned my prospective employer to explain that the Saturday I was to go for the interview. I was to have my last game for Leeds City Schoolboys. The man who was to become my employer didn't hesitate, he just said yes and make sure that you win, which we did.

These days were good, innocent days full of fun, full of comradeship and full of lessons about myself and others inside and outside the game. There was also the sheer joy of being so fit that my friends and I would play cricket, tennis and any other game we could. It was a time when in that working class culture there was a sense of belonging and sporting rivalry.

Days of innocence? Perhaps. They were also days of little choice, and they continued after school, as an apprentice electrician the wages for the first two years didn't meet expenses so fun had to be cheap and playing amateur rugby was both. We did what we had done as schoolboys. We changed at the side of the pitch and then went home on the bus in our muddy state. The exception to this norm was our home games when we had a shower at the youth club which we used as our base.

There was one final memory of my schoolboy rugby which stays with me. It is one of the teachers - all volunteers - who ran the Leeds City Schoolboys team. He was speaking after we had played a curtain raiser at Headingley. We were always invited to have a shower and a meal after the game by Leeds RLFC and on this occasion the teacher whose name escapes me (it was 50 years ago) advised the two teams present to remember that "professionalism" was perfectly acceptable and that while some of those present would become professionals, which they did, but the game itself was what was important.

Seeing some of the developments of recent times, such as arranging kick-off to meet television's needs, is putting the players and the game second. I am not saying that it is a seriously bad thing, certainly not a disaster, but it is another shift away from the happy innocence of playing Rugby League for school, club and country for the joy and the community you represent.

My thanks to everyone who helped to get me involved and to all of the fine friends I made when playing Rugby League.

Andy Burnham MP:
3 Next door but one to Mick Martyn

OK, I won't pretend. I'm a football man. Or to be more precise, I'm an Evertonian to the core - bitter-and-twisted, dyed-in-the-wool. So why, you are thinking, is he writing in a book like this?

Well, it's a fair question. My answer is that I come from, and now have the honour of representing, an area that is arguably Rugby League's strongest heartland. I just haven't been able to avoid the sport. I have played it, watched it and, ever since leaving home for university in 1988, defended it staunchly from attack in many a pub across the south of England.

Defending Rugby League came quite naturally because I've always treated attacks such as this as attacks on the north west and our way of life. But more than that, I've always liked the game and have never doubted its superiority to the other rugby code in just about every respect. Those prejudices were confirmed in me for life when I clapped eyes for the first time on the antics of the university Rugby Union club late one night in the college bar. But now my appreciation of Rugby League is moving beyond those gut reactions and, as my understanding grows, I'm learning to love it.

I was born in Liverpool in 1970 but one year later the family moved to Culcheth between Leigh and Warrington. To my mum and dad, Rugby League was a rural curiosity. They couldn't understand the fuss when Leigh fans would stop them in the shops and say: "Oooh, I hear you've moved in next door but one to Mick Martyn". Little did we know then that for us it would have been the equivalent of having Dixie Dean for a neighbour.

Mick and his family have been great friends to us over the years. My two brothers and I spent many long hours in our back garden playing football with Mick's son Stuart. Stuart's physical resemblance to his cousin Tommy, the St Helens star, is disturbing and in his early teens as expected he began to excel playing for Leigh Miners. But back-garden football and the odd trip to Goodison proved to be more enticing. To this day, we feel guilty for depriving Rugby League of his talents and hope Mick will forgive us one day.

Championship season

In the early 1980s, my brother Nick began playing for the Culcheth Lions RLFC. He would come home telling us how everyone was going to watch Leigh because they had a great team and a good chance of winning the league. So, in the season 1981-82, we started going to Hilton Park on a Sunday. "Glory-hunter", I hear you say. Well, you might be right. But bear in mind that at the time we were glory-starved young Everton fans. The joyous atmosphere of Hilton Park was a welcome contrast to those dark and broody Goodison Saturdays under the reign of Gordon Lee and the early days of Howard Kendall.

We probably went to six or seven games that championship season and I have vivid memories of the pin-point kicking of John Woods and the blinding pace of Des Drummond. We'd go home and tell my dad about the talents of these two. "Tell Kendall to get his cheque book out," he'd say.

We were there the day Leigh clinched the championship trophy and I remember running on the pitch before the trophy was paraded around the ground. But, for me, the most significant game of that season was the subsequent Premiership play-off at Hilton Park against Warrington. If I remember rightly, it was one drop-goal apiece. Purists will probably recall it now as the finest display of tackling and defensive organisation ever seen. But, for us, those drab 80 minutes meant the end of our temporary love affair with the game. And for those who were fond of saying at the time that the sport had no problem with hooliganism, we witnessed stark evidence to the contrary on the 587 bus back to Culcheth.

Playing the game

Those feelings of sheer panic on the 587 were to be repeated a few years later when I ran out on the pitch for my first competitive Rugby League game. My games teacher at school - St Aelred's Roman Catholic High in Newton-le-Willows - had become concerned at my wishy-washy approach to football. He saw the perfect cure - put me in the Rugby League team! And so it was that I began playing regularly. I've now had a few daunting experiences but don't think that anything will compare to being called off the bench on a cold January night in Wigan at St John Fisher. It was a baptism of fire - but one I enjoyed. Rugby League helped change my whole approach to football: you just couldn't go missing on the wing and expect your mates to talk to you afterwards. To my amazement, I found that timing a good tackle was actually quite satisfying.

At school, Rugby League and football were equally popular. In fact, League probably shaded it. There were more Saints fans than supporters of any other club, rugby or football. Some time in 1985, a Wigan 'pie-eater' mate of mine offered me an evens £10 bet after double geography that Rugby League would be bigger than football in 10 years. I took the bet, but only after a few minutes hesitation. That I had to think about it seems unbelievable today. But it is a measure of how much ground the game has lost in those 17 years.

The blame for its decline can be laid in many quarters. But there can be no doubt that it remains the victim of snobbery and the British establishment - and that includes the media establishment which, until Gazza cried at Italia '90, had treated football and football supporters in much the same disdainful way.

Football is now the official game of the media set. That its last 10 years have been a huge success story is taken as media fact. But I see it differently. Many developments in football have been for the worse. The breakaway by the FA Premier League and the end of financial redistribution as we knew it led, unsurprisingly, to a few clubs prospering at the expense of the wider game. Rampant greed in dressing-rooms and boardrooms was compounded by unscrupulous and incompetent club management and a lack of vision and teeth in the committee rooms of Lancaster Gate.

This is one view of football today. But much the same could be said of Rugby League. There are close parallels between the way football and Rugby League have developed since the establishment of the Premier League and Super League. Despite a huge influx of money, each game seems no better off.

But the similarities between the two go back further than that. When the northern rugby clubs started paying players, they set up as companies not because they sought to make a profit but because they had to limit the liabilities of their directors. Indeed, the Football Association has only recently removed rules which sought to resolve any conflict between sporting and business considerations. For many years, payments to directors were not allowed and football grounds could not be sold off or asset-stripped. But these rules were never enforced and as the money poured in to football, so did a whole host of disreputable wheelers and dealers attracted to the lack of regulation and accountability. Proud clubs built on generations of local support were turned into empty brands geared towards maximising returns to shareholders and to be cashed in on.

The future of football must lie in returning clubs to their community roots and I think the same is true of Rugby League.

I am the chair of an organisation called Supporters Direct, set up by the Government to promote greater supporter and community ownership of football clubs. It was based on the experience of Northampton Town FC. When that club went into administration in the early 1990s, a crisis meeting called by the fans decided not to raise money to throw into a black hole to prop up the regime that had already brought the club to the brink. Instead, they set up the Northampton Town Supporters' Trust. With the money raised, shares in the club were bought and, as new owners took over, a seat on the board was guaranteed for the elected head of the trust.

The trust's involvement in the club brought a range of benefits, from a 200 per cent increase in gates to the best facilities for disabled supporters in England, plus a vigorous anti-racism stance and football's first equal opportunities policy.

Supporters Direct has sought to replicate those benefits elsewhere by helping establish more than 60 mutual supporters' trusts across the country. With financial problems now gripping the lower leagues, it is an idea whose time has come. Now, supporters' trusts are beginning to emerge at Rugby League clubs - Bramley, Warrington, Swinton to name a few - and I believe they can have the same success in Rugby League, if not more.

The story of my own club sums up why it is necessary. I have heard from many different quarters how the building of Hilton Park was a real community effort. Everybody pitched in. For that simple reason, people see the club and its ground as the moral property of the people of Leigh and nothing else gives the town greater civic pride. And yet in the mid-1990s the club stood on the brink of extinction after financial problems.

It's the same sorry story wherever you look: Northern Ford Premiership, Nationwide League, Premier League or Super League. Clubs are being brought to their knees by greed and opportunism. Supporters' trusts are part of the fightback and give fans a proper voice in return for the financial and emotional investment they make in their clubs year after year.

We hope soon to extend the services of Supporters Direct to Rugby League. And when that happens, I believe the supporters' trusts movement could have a bigger impact on the sport than it has in football simply because the finances mean that trusts will not need to raise anything like as much to buy a significant stake in their clubs.

So in football and Rugby League, the tide is turning against 10 years of unhealthy commercialism and market values. Over the next 10, there needs to be far less emphasis on making a quick profit for the few and far more on nurturing the grassroots of both games that are becoming more run-down and impoverished with every year that passes. Given my background and interest in both games, nothing would give me greater pleasure than to play a part in this.

James Clappison MP:
4 A Robin and a Rhino

My father had many worthwhile interests but sport was not one of them. After a great deal of pressure he agreed to take me to watch Hull Kingston Rovers when I was about 12, during a Christmas holiday. Unfortunately it was a bitterly cold day and afterwards he pronounced that it had been even colder than on the sole occasion he had watched Hull City play Grimsby and even less interesting than our recent visit to the cinema to watch the Beatles' *Yellow Submarine* which, in retrospect, cannot have held much interest for an East Yorkshire farmer. I would not want to leave the impression that my father was in any way disobliging because this was far from the case. He did business with a butcher in Hull called Johnny Frankland who had been on the board of Hull KR and who lived in a neighbouring village and this was the solution, I went to Hull KR with him. Johnny was a kind man; I believe he was also a good butcher. It was an unimaginable treat for me to go into the Rovers boardroom for a half-time cup of tea with him.

Top dogs on Humberside

In the late 1960s Hull KR were going through one of the better periods in their history. They were definitely the top dogs on Humberside and were regularly around the top of the league, a state of affairs which had much to do with the arrival of Roger Millward from Castleford and the presence of internationals such as Phil Lowe and Peter "Flash" Flanagan. My hopes were highest when Rovers drew Leeds at home in the Challenge Cup quarter-final of the 1969-70 season. I remember great discussions at the time as to how more people could be packed into the ground and I was one of those fortunate enough to get a ticket. In it tense and exciting match Rovers emerged as 7-2 winners only to go out to Wigan in the semis, in a match I had to miss through being away at school. Wembley had to wait until the 1980 season and the famous (or infamous, depending on your allegiance) all-Humberside final. It was a great occasion - the greatest of Hull KR's history - but if one is to be objective, not one of the greatest finals. My most vivid memory is how the city of Hull took over the west end of London and peopled it with supporters in either red and white or black and white.

This is probably heresy, but I thought the 1982 Hull versus Widnes final at Wembley and the replay at Elland Road, both of which I attended, were better matches, the latter being remarkable for the fact that 39,000 out of a 40,000 crowd seemed to come from Hull. However, neither were what I regard as my all time great matches, which I will come to a in moment. There were many great matches and finals involving the Humberside teams in the early 1980s. Hull has always been a rugby town, but in the 1980s somehow it caught the imagination of the city and the surrounding area in a way it had never done before. Both clubs produced great teams and recruited overseas stars such as Hull FC's Kemble, Leuluai, O'Hara and Sterling and Rovers' Broadhurst, Gordon Smith, Miller and Dorahy.

By now I was working as a Leeds barrister and in a position to follow Hull KR both home and away. The 1985-86 cup run stands out among many great memories. After an improbable 2-0 away victory over St Helens in the first round I remember driving back across the Pennines in the thickest fog I have ever experienced. The first semi-final against Leeds at Elland Road was probably the finest match I have ever seen. Twelve man Hull KR showed terrific team spirit to earn a replay through a 24-24 draw in a match which swung one way and then another. I missed the replay which Hull KR won comfortably as a result of a previously arranged holiday in Bruges - this is a problem with unforeseen replays.

1986 Challenge Cup Final

The 1986 final against Castleford was something of a disappointment; Hull KR had a chance to win the match through a last-minute kick from the injured John Dorahy, but the kick went wide and the consensus was that they probably didn't deserve to win. Besides being a little disappointed that final was something of a watershed for Hull KR. The two league titles of 1984 and 1985 became distant memories as the club slipped down the table and even suffered the ignominy of relegation. For a time the financial survival of the club was in question and the club moved to New Craven Park. It was the misfortune of Hull KR to be going through a bad period in its history when the Super League era arrived with its tendency to institutionalise the gap between the haves and the have-nots.

In the meantime the arrival of a family and election to Parliament changed my circumstances. My son is a keen Rugby League supporter - his own decision - and follows Leeds. The first match his father took him to was a 33-28 Leeds victory over Wigan; after a start like that it was hardly surprising that Henry became a committed fan. Over recent years I have accompanied him to Leeds matches home and away, while paying occasional visits to watch Hull KR. Leeds are a good club who have worked hard at forging a relationship with their supporters. Given the scale of their support and the calibre of their playing staff it is a mystery to me why they have not won more. I had the privilege of watching them in the last Wembley final and the first Murrayfield final, both memorable occasions, the first because Leeds actually managed to win the Challenge Cup and the second because it was a terrific occasion albeit a disappointing game.

I get the same thrill and enjoyment from watching Rugby League now as I did when I was a boy. It is hard to put my finger on exactly what draws me to Rugby league. I also enjoy watching football and Rugby Union, but for me there will always be something special about Rugby League. It is vastly underrated as a game. Some sections of the media do not give it a fair crack of the whip, but that is more of a reflection on them then it is on Rugby League. Whether watching Hull KR, Leeds or any other club, I have never been to a match which I did not find enjoyable and I suspect I never will.

Above: Lord Jack Ashley (Photo: Courtesy Lord Jack Ashley)
Below: Andy Burnham MP (right) with Mick Martyn at Hilton Park
(Photo: Courtesy Andy Burnham)

Yvette Cooper MP:
5 Coming to terms with Tiger Town

Thirty school children clutch their coloured streamers. The band starts up, the majorettes twirl their pom-poms, and the town's jubilee heritage festival is about to begin with a maypole parade. Shouldering the head of the maypole is a man in a stripy tiger suit and rugby shorts.

Anywhere else, the site of a cuddly tiger leading the maypole through the main street would be a little surreal. In Castleford, no-one bats an eyelid. Indeed no one is better placed to lead the parade of the town's pride than the mascot of the local Tigers Rugby League team. Castleford is passionate about its Rugby League team. And the Tigers repay that passion and that loyalty with a community focus rarely rivalled among top sports clubs.

Sir Jack Smart [former leader of Wakefield Council] took me to my first match at Wheldon Road. Selected unexpectedly from their final candidates shortlist by the local Labour Party just a few days before, I had been thrown into a flurry of campaigning. The election was imminent, and dripping with rosettes we had visited two factories and a street stall already that day. Jack said he would try to fix it for me to say a few words to the crowd before the match started, so I paced the touchline nervously rehearsing a few short sentences - what do you say to a large crowd who just want to watch the rugby?

My moment came. The compere – dressed in an Elvis suit – introduced me to the crowd. Then to my horror, instead of being given the microphone, I was given the ball. He announced: "Today's match will be kicked off by Labour's candidate for Pontefract and Castleford: Yvette Cooper." Composing a suitable sound-bite was suddenly a doddle, faced with the prospect of kicking a rugby ball in front of thousands of people. And I was in heels. Mortified, I looked down at my long straight skirt and wobbly shoes and tottered onto the pitch. I didn't think I could kick a rugby ball, never mind kick it and stay upright. Nor could I see any possible way out. I took a deep breath and braced myself for the prospect that thousands of potential voters were going to get the first sight of their Labour candidate as she slipped straight on her behind. Even worse, what if I missed the ball altogether?

I gritted my teeth and booted the ball as hard as I could down the pitch. Amazingly I remained standing, and didn't rip my skirt. It wasn't a bad kick. The crowd clapped politely. My dignity was almost intact. The trouble was I was so overwhelmed with relief that I couldn't remember what I was supposed to do next. I stood in the middle of the pitch in a daze. Then suddenly it occurred to me that these 26 burly men - 13 behind me, 13 in front - might be about to start chasing the ball. And I was in the way. Convinced that the match had now actually started and that I was about to be squashed, I started running to the stand at breakneck speed. My husband Ed looked on in horror from the stands. So much for dignity. The match itself was a bit of a blur after that and unfortunately my kick did not end Castleford's bad start to that season. We lost to Warrington 24-8. I was elected MP 17 days later.

Hailing from the smallest town in Super League, Castleford Tigers don't have the money and international buying power of the bigger clubs. Castleford's population is only around 39,000, compared to more than 700,000 in Leeds, almost 80,000 in Wigan and 62,000 in Wakefield. But the club makes up for it in community strength and persistence. Youth teams and training programmes nurture new talent. And we are ever optimistic that a flash of brilliance might slip them through to the cup or nudge them into the play-offs.

Semi-final

Three years ago, watching the Tigers take on the London Broncos in the semi-final of the Challenge Cup at Leeds, I thought we were moments away from a place at Wembley for the Cup final. After a dodgy first 20 minutes, Castleford fought back from 14-2 down. Four tries later, we were catching up. Then a spectacular back pass from Adrian Vowles set up the fifth try from Michael Eagar to take Castleford into the lead just eight minutes from the end. Another try from the Broncos and a drop goal from Danny Orr took the score to 27-all. But then in a devastating blow to the thousands of Castleford supporters all biting our lips, our players seemed to try to juggle the ball in the air, London's Steele Retchless grabbed it to score the final Broncos try with just seconds to go. So near and yet so far.

For 30 years, Castleford have sustained their position in the top division of British Rugby League. While pits have closed, ski slopes are opening, and much about the town has changed beyond recognition, the club still goes on. In 1994, Castleford won the Regal Trophy and ran a close run against Wigan in the Premiership final. Matches are still played down at Wheldon Road, home to the club since the 1920s.

Of course the club has reflected many of the changes in the town. Castleford Rugby League Club has become Castleford Tigers. For over 10 years to the mid-nineties, the club's sponsor was Hicksons & Welch, the chemical company opposite the ground that has stood in the town for over 80 years. Now, the sponsors are jungle.com – an internet based company selling computers and other high-tech equipment. Green foam hands have joined scarves and ever changing kit colours as the must-haves for each game. The arrival of Sky television and the Super League has raised the razzmatazz. Tiger Tot and JT join Tiger Man on mini- mopeds around the ground alongside balloons, sirens and the video referee. And, of course, instead of freezing on a foggy January afternoon, we can enjoy a balmy (sometimes) summer evening match instead.

Castleford's Tiger
(Photo: Peter Lush)

On match days in Castleford the entire town turns out. Thousands of orange shirts flood down Bridge Street and along Wheldon Road. Young men spill out from the pubs. Teenage girls gather with their mates. Couples sport identical team shirts from last season. Grey haired men take their six-year-old granddaughters. Wave after wave they come, past the bus station, past Hicksons, past Nestlé, past the man with the bucket collecting for the hospice. The crowd averages 7,000, most from Castleford. More people in the town went to the last match than turned out to vote in Castleford in the May local elections. The shouts and sirens can be heard right across town. If we miss a match on a Sunday, we can hear from our garden in Redhill whether the team is winning or not by the size of the cheers.

For us it really is a family event. Most people wouldn't consider taking a toddler to a Premiership football match. But Ed took our daughter to her first Rugby League match aged 18 months and she loved it - our son did even better starting at nine months.

We sit up in the stands with supplies of chips, doughnuts and small toys to keep them entertained if their interest wanes. Dean Sampson is wrestled to the ground by a Salford Red. At not quite three years old, our daughter hollers: "Get off him. Get off him." Danny Orr scores a try. We all sing: "Danny boy, Danny boy." Darren Rogers does a long run down the left side and we're all on the edge of our seats. Tom from across the aisle points out that our toddler is crawling up the steep steps towards the reporters. I rescue her and miss the try.

Yvette Cooper MP at Castleford Tigers versus Warrington Wolves
(Photo: Courtesy Yvette Cooper MP)

Matches at the Jungle are great family and community events. But the club's role in the community stretches way beyond match day. Ever conscious of their dependence on the town for support, the club and the players repay the loyalty of the town by, in turn, supporting the community. Fund raising events, community pride days, whatever the occasion, never be surprised to see a Tiger there. They are often in local schools, supporting sports events, promoting fitness and healthy eating among children. They joined a local partnership with the British Heart Foundation and the local Primary Care Group to prevent heart disease – one of the biggest killers in the area. They support literacy and numeracy summer schools for local children. And they even involve local schools and children in the half time entertainment.

When the match is over, the town trails home. Fifteen abreast we walk back down Wheldon Road. Those who made the mistake of trying to get their car too close to the ground are stuck crawling behind lines of pedestrians. If we win or lose, the crowd is good-humoured and will be back. Castleford Rugby League Club has been inspiring its town for nearly 80 years. It will keep on doing so for at least 80 more.

6 Tony Cunningham MP: Workington Town at Old Trafford

On a bridge over the A66 just past Cockermouth someone had draped a banner proclaiming: "Last one out, knock the lights off!" West Cumbria was on the road, a mass exodus of rugby league fans of the Workington Town persuasion to watch their favourites in action at one of the country's most famous stadiums - Old Trafford.

The date - 21 May 1994 - one of the biggest dates in the history of the proud club from Cumbria, who many thought would never savour another moment like this. Town's golden era had been the 1950s when they won the Challenge Cup at Wembley and the Championship at Maine Road. They reached two more Challenge Cup finals in 1955 and 1958 but finished as runners-up on both occasions. Workington had won the short-lived Western Division Championship in 1962 and in a magical spell in the mid 1970s reached four successive Lancashire Cup finals, winning the second in 1977.

But in the late 1980s and early 1990s Town looked to be in permanent decay. Gates had fallen to below 500 and Workington found themselves in the newly-formed Third Division. That was the lowest point in the club's history. At the foot of the League and with only four wins and two draws from 28 games, Town had reached rock bottom.

Then, for the start of the 1992-93 season enter stage left a new coach, Australian Peter Walsh, and the start of a remarkable run which saw the Cumbrians rise from the depths to the heights in less than three years.

Walsh had played in England with Oldham but was hardly a big name, and had no real coaching experience. But when he left the club he had carved out a special place in Town's history books as the fans flocked back to Derwent Park to give the team some of their best support for many years.

The new coach led Town to second place in the Third Division in his first season in charge, and for good measure took them to Old Trafford for the Premiership final where they lost 20-16 to Featherstone Rovers. It was all good experience for what was to follow 12 months later in what was undoubtedly Town's finest season of the modern era.

Town produced some magical moments for their fans in the 1993-94 season. They won the Second Division championship amidst memorable scenes at Bramley, after which skipper Colin Armstrong was presented with the trophy before he disappeared under a sea of Workington fans who had made the trip to Leeds.

The west Cumbrians won the title by a point from Doncaster, who in turn were just a point ahead of London Crusaders - but more of them later. Town scored 760 points in 30 matches - not as many as London who scored 842, but significantly they had the League's tightest defence, conceding just 331.

In the first round of the end-of-season Premiership, Town swept to a 50-6 home win over Rochdale and although the semi-final was a lot tighter, they won it 19-4 over Batley to set up the second successive trip to Old Trafford for the Workington faithful.

It seemed everyone who was anybody in Workington made the trip that day and they were rewarded with an uplifting display by Peter Walsh's men.

A pulsating performance by the west Cumbrians, particularly in the first half, helped add the divisional crown to the League title they won at Bramley a few weeks earlier. The classic confrontation of north versus south, with two of Rugby League's outposts represented at the Old Trafford showpiece, made for a hugely entertaining contest.

That the Crusaders were put to the sword was mainly down to Town's intense effort over the opening 40 minutes, which established an interval lead of 24-6. The Londoners finished the half demoralised, cut to ribbons by a rampant Workington team, which threatened to turn the final into a one-sided romp.

It was to the Crusaders' credit that, without key players hooker Scot Carter and scrum-half Mark Riley for all but the first 15 minutes of the game, both players being injured, they came back to make a contest of it in the second half. Town, who had to show their defensive qualities after the break, were grateful for several unforced errors by the Crusaders, but nevertheless needed a late try from Stuart Cocker to eventually put the game beyond the Londoners' reach.

Game plan

Before the game Walsh had said he thought his side could win comfortably if they got the first score on the board. Weathering London's early storm, trying to take the match to the Crusaders and taking them on up-front was a condensed version of the Walsh game plan. And it certainly went according to plan in the first half. Given a rapturous reception by the blue army of travelling fans, Town were given a flier by Ged Byrne after only five minutes. Byrne had made the best comeback since Lazarus to make the starting line-up. Devastated after a shoulder injury the previous week, there looked to be no way he would be fit in time to play his farewell game on the Old Trafford stage.

But he made it, after several days of intense treatment, and his coach's faith in selecting him for the big game wasn't down to sentiment as the

Workington Town versus London Crusaders - Old Trafford May 1994
(Photo: David Williams)

opening try demonstrated. Byrne, who had started his professional career 13 years ago two miles across the city in Salford, turned the clock back to his schoolboy sprinting days as he went down the touchline on a 30-yard burst for the line. Somehow the loose-forward evaded all the challenges that were made and dived over for the score, which Walsh and his team wanted.

What wasn't in the script was London's riposte on eight minutes. Skipper Sam Stewart's little kick through evaded Des Drummond and South African ace winger Mark Johnson (who was to sign for Town in 1995) was there to touch down. John Gallagher's conversion went over via the crossbar.

It took Workington just five minutes to regain the lead. Stand-off Wayne Kitchin broke through and then quick hands by Phil McKenzie and Byrne put Tony Kay striding through for the second try which Dean Marwood converted. A Marwood penalty on 18 minutes stretched Town's lead to 12-6 and London looked vulnerable. With the influential Riley back in the dressing room along with Carter, the Londoners were sadly lacking in a key area of the field and Town made them pay.

Stuart Cocker fittingly chose the Old Trafford stage to show why he's regarded in Workington as the Jimmy Greaves of Rugby League - a sniffer-out of half chances. There seemed to be no danger after 24 minutes when

Marwood hoisted a huge kick from just inside his own half and slanted it for the left-hand comer.

Andre Stoop and Gallagher should have covered the danger but the ever-alert Cocker first out-ran the former All Black and then just got his fingertips there first to beat Stoop to the touchdown.

James Pickering, a colossus at prop for Town, was having a big first half for the Cumbrians and on the half hour, one of his bullocking runs released Kitchin. He had support either side but ran into defenders as he elected to go it alone.

The attacking potion had been established, however, and two minutes later Town scored their fourth try. Marwood, who went on to win the Tom Bergin Trophy as man of the match, snatched-up a loose ball from a scrum and broke through the initial London cover. Kitchin was first there in support and his well-timed pass put Drummond galloping over in the comer. Four minutes from the break Town's fans were on their feet again, this time as Mark Mulligan came through to round-off more pressure on the London line. Kay did well to slip the ball from the tackle and the Australian full-back made no mistake.

Tony Gordon's half-time team talk would have made interesting listening but whatever was said there was more determination and direction about the Crusaders' play in the second half. Town were forced back for long periods and earned high praise for their defensive work, scrambling across in both comers to deny Johnson and Gallagher.

The Town pack played like lions, especially Pickering and Brad Hepi, tackling feverishly in the second period when London played their best rugby. They held them until the 66th minute when the impressive Stoop came surging through to put Johnson at the comer and Gallagher converted impressively. Town were still comfortably ahead, but in danger of allowing London to get up a late head of steam, so they needed a score to settle the nerves and put the game beyond their rivals.

Midfield break

It came after 73 minutes, and stemmed from another surging midfield break by Pickering. Byrne, only back on the field two minutes for the injured Kay, took over and just when he seemed he was going to end his career with a try-double, sensed Cocker could finish more comfortably and gave the winger a clear run-in.

Marwood's conversion had surely finished-off the Crusaders? But no, the London fight-back continued with two more tries in the last four minutes. Stoop took a wicked bomb from Mulligan just outside his own 22 and then proceeded to race almost right through the Workington team on a brilliant counter-attack, which eventually had its reward when Logan Campbell (another who was to join Town later) sliced through for the try, which Gallagher converted.

Still the Crusaders weren't finished. More London pressure saw Stoop surge into the line to provide Johnson with his hat-trick in the comer. But it was too little, too late.

Walsh, who signed a two year contract with Town almost immediately after the game, said: "It was very rewarding to go back to Old Trafford after a defeat in the final and put the record straight second time round. The players really stuck to the script we had prepared and we had the game won by halftime.

"We had been so much on top during the first half that we did lose the plot a little in - the second half but we had enough in reserve to win with a bit to spare."

Workington Town: Mulligan, Drummond, Kay (Byrne 71), Bums, Cocker, Kitchin, Marwood, Pickering, Riley (46), McKenzie, Armstrong (Pickering 60), Hepi, Oglanby, Byrne (Penrice 50).
Tries: Byrne, Kay, Cocker (2), Drummond, Mulligan. Goals: Marwood (3).
London Crusaders: Stoop, Gallagher, Roskell, Campbell, Johnson, McIvor, Riley (Luxon 13), Whiteley, Carter (Smith 6), Rotheram, Rosolen, Stewart, Ramsey.
Tries: Johnson (3), Campbell. Goals: Gallagher (3).

Workington Town versus London Crusaders -
Old Trafford May 1994 (Photo: David Williams)

Workington's victory at Old Trafford (Photo: David Williams)

Frank Dobson MP:
A Clarence Street boy

Wembley, May Day 1999. It's a great moment in my life. I am about to present the Rugby League Challenge Cup to Leeds Rhinos who have just beaten London Broncos in the final. Leeds' captain Iestyn Harris is reaching out for the cup and I am clutching it so tight my knuckles are white. It would be a pity to drop the lovely old trophy which means so much to Rugby League players and followers. But I have a more selfish reason for holding it tight. Leeds have just scored a record 52 points, have won by a record margin of 36, Leroy Rivett has scored a record four tries and Iestyn Harris a record-equalling eight goals. I want the 1999 final, the last at the old Wembley, to be remembered for the brilliant rugby played that day. I am desperate for it not to go down in history as the match where "that daft prat with a beard dropped the cup."

Anyway, between us, Iestyn and I managed the hand over without mishap and I handed out the winners' medals. All the Leeds players looked knackered - apart from Leroy who was so psyched-up he looked as if he could easily have played another 80 minutes and scored another four tries.

Before that, I had presented the losers' medals to the London Broncos. They looked close to death - bodies wracked by the physical exertion, hopes dashed by the result, pride shattered by the scale of their defeat. It was horrible. They had been in the lead for most of the first half, and still in the game until the last 20 minutes. Men who, for years, had graced our game, displaying spell-binding skill, unmatched pace and awesome commitment, couldn't bear to look people in the eye. They were so hurt, it was painful to watch.

It must have been worst for Shaun Edwards. He held the record for appearances in Wembley finals; and up to then had always been on the winning side. More often than not he had made the difference between winning and losing. This time, his last Wembley appearance, he had lost. And it was physically painful as well. Shaun had broken his thumb in the semi-final and wouldn't have a pain-killing jab for the final. But, like many a Rugby League star before him, he had played his heart out no matter what the pain.

It really was a remarkable honour to present the cup at Wembley. I had been quite a few times before - I liked the old stadium. It's a bit of a dump, but it's a romantic dump.

Meeting the teams on the pitch before the kick-off was a strange experience. When you are introduced to the players, most of them aren't really there. They shake your hand, but their minds are elsewhere. They are concentrating so hard on the game to come. It's called "getting your priorities right".

I've seen some wonderful games at Wembley. After I moved from York to London my first visit to Wembley for a Rugby League Challenge Cup Final was to see Wakefield Trinity wallop Hull in 1960. The night before I had observed a lone Hull supporter with scarf and rosette lying drunk in the gloom against the railings in Tavistock Square moaning quietly "They said London was bloody lively".

The 1961 final between St Helens and Wigan was a classic and included the best try I've ever seen. I can still. see it in my mind's eye. Ken Large and Tom van Vollenhoven interpassed for 90 yards before the South African touched down. There was also a funny incident that afternoon. Three St Helens players went to tackle the great Billy Boston. A lass from Wigan behind me shouted "Tha' leave our Billy alone". By the time she had finished voicing her concern "our Billy" was back on his feet - unlike two of his tacklers who had clashed heads and needed attention.

In the early 1960s the two ends at Wembley were open to the sky, the concrete terracing was always cold and often wet - so everybody had to stand to watch. At one final, I can't remember which, it was very hot and sunny. The concrete was warm and dry so before the game we all sat down in the sun.

When the band played the National Anthem, common sense prevailed over patriotism. Everybody instinctively understood that if anybody stood up, that was it for the rest of the afternoon. So everybody sat tight and Wembley, that afternoon, became an informal all-seater stadium.

Other Wembley Rugby League memories that stick in my mind include poor Don Fox missing the last kick of the game in front of the posts to give Leeds a one point victory in 1968. But the most memorable, without a doubt, was in 1990 when Ellery Hanley, the finest player I've ever watched, led Great Britain to their 19-12 victory over Australia. And lead he did. That match had everything: skill, speed, power, commitment, tension and best, of all, a Great Britain win. The following week, I was talking to Dennis Howell, who had been our most famous Sports Minister. He'd seen it all. He'd reffed an FA Cup Final. He wasn't a rugby man, he was football through and through. But he told me that rugby test was the most exciting sporting event he'd ever witnessed.

Mind you, I wasn't the first in my family to watch Rugby League at Wembley. I come from a Rugby League family. We supported York. When I was growing up, York weren't exactly a top-flight club. So I was intrigued

York in the 1950s: Basil Watts back row, first left, Jim Bowden, back row sixth left, Brian Smith, seated extreme right.
(Photo: Courtesy Robert Gate)

Wembley 1999 Challenge Cup Final.

Iestyn Harris holds the Cup - Frank Dobson MP can be seen behind the Cup.
(Photo: David Williams)

one day to come across an old, worn and faded crepe paper black and amber rosette. I was then doubly astonished to discover it had been worn by my mother at Wembley in 1931 when York lost to Halifax. First, I didn't know York had ever made the final. Second, I didn't know my mother had ever been a fan. And I also learned that Halifax were not well thought of in the Dobson household because their forwards had handed out a series of injuries to the York backs in a league game shortly before the final.

First game

I can easily pinpoint the first Rugby League game I saw. It was York versus St Helens on 20 September 1947. I remember very clearly who York played because, in all innocence, I thought they were playing St Helen's Church, not a major industrial town in Lancashire. And I know which year it was because in those days, the Yorkshire sides didn't get to play the leading Lancashire sides every season. St Helens didn't visit York again until 1950 and I was attending regularly by then. I don't remember a thing about the game, but I do recall going to the old Clarence Street ground. I had been there before, to see the Russian Cossacks performing all sorts of impressive feats with sabres and lances from the backs of their stocky-looking horses.

So, that was how it started. After that I went fairly regularly with my dad and later with my big brother Geoff. The next incident I clearly remember is York being slaughtered by Wigan. Ken Gee kicked one conversion which bounced on the crossbar and went over. Some spectators shouted "do it again" and, lo and behold, whether by design or accident, he did.

My dad brought me up to appreciate the skilful play of stand-offs, centres and wingers rather than the tricky activity of scrum-halves. Gus Risman was his idea of how a rugby player should play and how decent men should live their lives. Gus had played before the Second World War for Salford. And after Workington Town joined the RFL in 1945-46 he captained them to victory in the Championship in 1951 and the Cup in 1952. My dad also really admired some of the players from Australia and New Zealand. His favourites were Huddersfield's Australian winger Lionel Cooper and Wigan's New Zealander Cec Mountford.

York signed a New Zealander, Johnny Robinson, a stand-off who was pretty good in attack and the best tackling back I ever saw. He played some representative games for the overseas players' side Other Nationalities.

That may have been one reason why my dad took me to Hull in 1951 to see Other Nationalities play a world-beating French Side at The Boulevard. But it wasn't the skilled play that sticks in the memory. First of all, my dad bought me some roast chestnuts from a seller outside the ground. Then, when the Marseillaise was played, he and all the other men took off their trilbies or flat caps. Then there was an outburst of violence on the pitch. The French second-rowers, Brousse and Ponsinet were hard men, known as the terrible twins. Ponsinet had clashed in an earlier game with Leeds's Australian second-row, Arthur Clues, who himself was a sort of one-man terrible twin. Ponsinet had come off worst in the previous game and decided to get his retaliation in first. He laid out Clues with one mighty wallop and, unless my memory is playing tricks on me, didn't even wait to be sent off. His absence, no doubt, contributed to the downfall of France that afternoon. I also remember being riveted by the sight of Puig-Aubert, the French captain and goalkicker. Instead of carefully placing the ball so it pointed towards the goal he just plonked it down with the long axis parallel to the goal and booted it over.

Goal-kicking

Strange but effective methods of goal-kicking were not the monopoly of the French. As I got into my teens, I used to go to see York with a lad who had relatives in Barrow. So we paid special attention when they visited. They were a real power in the land in those days with two athletic muscular and talented centres, Jackson and Goodwin. Their skipper, stand-off, goalkicker and inspiration was Willie Horne. He kicked goals with his instep. That seemed ok for shots in front of goal but looked impossible for attempts from the touchline. We watched Willie achieve the impossible.

For much of the 1950s, York did not have a great deal of success. Sometimes, along with Liverpool Stanley and Rochdale Hornets, we adorned the bottom few places of that long, long league table. In addition to Johnny Robinson we did have some good players including a forward called Basil Watts. Considering the working-class backbone of Rugby League, a player called Basil playing at a ground called Clarence doesn't sound very macho, but Baz was. Had he been playing for a better side, he might well have got more than his five caps for Great Britain.

We went to see him in 1955 playing against New Zealand at Odsal. He made a solid contribution to the defeat of the visitors. Odsal, true to form, was a mud bath. By half-time, the teams were indistinguishable. Both appeared to be playing in the black of New Zealand. Great Britain, who were not supposed to be playing in black, had to change their kit at half time. The one exception to all this was Lewis Jones whom Leeds had signed from Welsh Rugby Union for the then amazing sum of £6,000. He had scarcely a mark on his shirt. Never a wild enthusiast for tackling, his contribution came in bursts. He saved himself for the second half. The others changed shirts. He changed gear.

Despite being brought up to value the elegant ball players, like most other Rugby League followers, I really can't restrain the regard I have for the way our players put aside pain and injury for the sake of their side. It's a hard game.

It had its heroes then. It has them now. But none can match Alan Prescott playing on, against the Australians in the Brisbane test in 1958, with a broken arm. He decided he could bear the pain better than he could bear the thought of further reducing to 11 men the side he was captaining against the Aussies. The Lions went on to win with 12 men.

I remember seeing close-up how another Great Britain forward coped with pain. Tommy Harris, the Hull hooker was playing at York. Somebody kicked him in the face. It was accidental, not deliberate, but a boot is a boot. He stumbled to the touch line right in front of us. The trainer came up with galvanised bucket and magic sponge, rummaged around in Tommy's mouth and threw several dislodged teeth into the bucket. I felt awful just watching. But the man himself grabbed the sponge, rinsed his mouth out, tossed back the sponge to join his teeth in the bucket and returned to the field to play a blinder.

Most spectators watch sport for the excitement of the competition. That's why exhibition games are less attractive.

We also go to admire the levels of skill, speed and strength we wish we had. We certainly know that. the endurance and ability to absorb pain and injury displayed in professional Rugby League are well beyond our personal thresholds. But I think most of us also get a thrill from the sheer brute force; usually within the rules and sometimes not. My mother was just short of being a pacifist. Her comment when she learnt of the atomic bomb at Hiroshima was "They were all somebody's bairns". But she also loved recalling how a visitor to Clarence Street called Saddington was laid out by a clearly delivered upper-cut from a York player. My mother always chortled as she explained that when he came round he asked "Who kicked me?"

It really is a tough game. I've mentioned a few painful incidents but it's always hard, with some of the most fragile-looking players having to take a terrible pounding match after match throughout their careers.

One example was Warrington's Brian Bevan. He looked as though he had been sent home from a TB sanatorium to die - until he got the ball and a minimum of space. He had enormous speed and an uncanny ability to evade tackles. But he couldn't evade them all and when he took a real cruncher you wondered whether he would ever get up again, let alone score a match-winning try minutes later. But he could and he did. It's not just the brutes who are hard in Rugby League. They are all harder than the rest of us.

The York side in that period included a few people who stick in my memory. We had a winger called Tate. In his day job he was a copper. Not always quick off the mark, his detractors called him Hesi Tate - obvious, even if unfair. York's most successful player at that time was Vic Yorke, prop and goal-kicker. He notched up a club career record of more than 1,000 goals including around 150 in the 1956-57 season. He never became an international, but was capped by Yorkshire and scored a bag full of goals for the county at Clarence Street against the visiting New Zealanders.

The player with the most appearances for York was full-back Willie Hargreaves. He was the subject of a persistent rumour - urban myth these days. In fact there were two stories. Both started with him being out of form one game because he was feeling queasy. The plain version went that his wife had fed him a tin of cat food by mistake. The less politically-correct version was that this deed was done deliberately by his mother-in-law.

One odd incident sticks in my mind. In York in those days at half-time they left a rugby ball on the field and a motley collection of younger kids jumped over the fence to play with it during the interval. None wore sports kit. Imagine the surprise one afternoon when this interlude was enlivened by a much bigger and older blond-haired lad in full rugby kit who grabbed the ball and made spectacular try-scoring runs. What made it even more surprising for me was that he was a classmate from Archbishop Holgate's School whose playing fields were just across the road. I believe he went on to be a successful hospital doctor.

Needless to say, we played Rugby Union at my grammar school. But we all watched Rugby League and couldn't be insulated from its influence. One of my younger playing colleagues at that time was Geoff Wriglesworth who later played Rugby League for Leeds and Great Britain. At school he was a centre or winger with a high stepping run which made him dangerous to tackle - a task I never faced because I never played against him - what a relief.

Once I moved to London, I only got to Clarence Street occasionally - going with my brother if York were playing at home on a weekend when I was in town. On one occasion, our young daughter was with us when a man called Naughton was abused by name throughout most of the game. She couldn't see his name on either team sheet. So I had to explain. He was the ref. One day York were playing Hunslet. They appeared to be playing in red, green and white. But there was nothing pedestrian about Hunslet. The official team sheet description of their colours was myrtle, flame and silver.

I was saddened when York moved from Clarence Street to the new Ryedale Stadium. This year [2002] I have been even more saddened because they have gone bust and lost their place in the league. Thankfully, the efforts to relaunch the club have succeeded and York will take up their place again in the RFL.

I owe a debt of gratitude to York Rugby League. They introduced me to my favourite sport. They set me on a course which has brought me immense pleasure, appreciation, excitement and amusement. Without them I would never have had the remarkable honour of presenting the Challenge Cup at Wembley. That's why, as I sat there in the Royal Box, I thought wistfully about being taken by my dad all those years ago to see York play St Helens. I wondered what he, my mother and my brother would have thought about me presenting the cup. I like to think they would have been pleased. I'm sure they would have been amazed.

David Hinchliffe MP: It was nothing to do with a missed conversion

I have a black and white photograph on the wall of my office given to me by former Trinity winger, John Etty, showing him scoring for Wakefield against Hull in the 1960 Championship semi-final at Belle Vue. In the background, at the front of a packed crowd, are a group of young lads clinging to their positions where the bottom of the terrace meets the edge of the field. I am there in the middle, perched on the wall at the side of the pitch, half turning to see him cross the line.

That picture encapsulates so much of a childhood and adolescence spent in the company of the best team (so far) in Wakefield Trinity's long and distinguished history. I witnessed first hand the great era of Neil Fox, of Harold Poynton and Keith Holliday, of Jack Wilkinson, Don Vines and Derek Turner and all the other great names of our famous cup-winning sides.

As a youngster it was necessary to be at our Belle Vue ground not long after the gates were opened at 1.00pm on a Saturday afternoon to stand any chance of getting in a position to be able to see at the regular kick off time of 3.00pm. On more than one occasion in the late fifties and early sixties I left the ground without my feet touching the ground, jammed between two or more adults as the crowd surged out at just turned 4.30pm.

On one occasion some fool had parked a London style taxi immediately outside the main spectator exit at the side of the old West Stand at the end of a particular match. The crowd poured out of the ground pressing a number of children against the vehicle and causing some distress. With minimal fuss several large men held back the crowd while someone opened the passenger door ushering any number of us in one side and safely out of the other.

There were big crowds in that period of great success, but rarely any bother. If there was any trouble it was usually on the field and as kids I recall we were deeply impressed when the fisticuffs broke out. With packs containing the likes of Wilkinson, Vines and Turner, I witnessed some mighty confrontations, none more so than in 1963 when the Australian tourists beat Trinity 29-14 in front of nearly 16,000 people at Belle Vue. Towards the end of the match, Trinity's Brian Briggs was laid out in the scrum by a Kangaroo forward and an all out brawl ensued involving all but a couple of players out on the wing. Wags in the crowd called for their dismissal for failing to join in.

Shortly after the referee had warned both sides with dismissal threats, Briggs was subjected to a high tackle by Australian captain Ian Walsh resulting in Trinity skipper Turner throwing a punch. After the referee had stepped between Walsh and Turner, Walsh was ordered off but appeared to refuse to go. When he eventually went, he was involved in a confrontation with an angry spectator and the police had to intervene. Rumours persist that both sides were still at it during the subsequent civic reception!

It was years later, when I read Ian Head's book *The Kangaroos*, that I learned why Walsh had taken what, in Rugby League, was the unheard of step of defying the referee. Heads claimed the referee had pointed to Walsh and said "Get off Kelly" (Noel Kelly being another Kangaroo front rower). Walsh had resisted, saying he wasn't Kelly.

I have other reasons for memories of the flare-ups in a much more recent match. The fortunes of Wakefield Trinity RLFC since the victory over Featherstone Rovers in the Division One Grand Final in 1998 have been a roller coaster ride of joy and despair for their fans, with the latter being the predominant emotion. Against a widespread belief amongst Trinity supporters that the Super League powers-that-be never wanted their team in the elite division in the first place, the club plunged the depths of entering a creditors voluntary agreement because of financial difficulties and suffering points reductions for an alleged breach of the salary cap. The chief executive apparently left the country and some important questions about this period in Trinity's history remain very much unanswered.

Dunkirk spirit

Despite these and numerous other worrying off-field events, coach John Harbin had done a remarkable job of fostering a Dunkirk spirit in the dressing room. The ultimate test was in the last round of the 2001 season when, after losing 21-19 to a resurgent Huddersfield Giants at Belle Vue the previous week, Trinity faced Salford at the Willows. Huddersfield were at home to London Broncos on the same day with a slightly earlier kick-off time. If they won and Wakefield lost, Trinity would be relegated.

As Salford took a 24-14 lead, the Willows electronic scoreboard informed the 2,000 strong away contingent at the opposite end of the ground that Huddersfield were coasting to a comfortable victory over London. With relegation staring Trinity in the face, the second half of that match was probably one of the most dramatic the game is likely to produce.

There had been some 'feeling' in the first half and both sides had ended the half down to 12 men after Trinity's Martin Pearson and Salford's

Malcolm Alker had been sin-binned following the first brawl of the match. The Trinity fans were incensed when, after one of the Salford tries, former Wakefield player Bobbie Goulding - one of several owed money by the club for the 2000 season - t appeared to gesture at them.

The second half began with Neil Law going over in the corner for Wakefield after a move involving Brad Davis and Justin Brooker. Pearson - back from the sin-bin - converted the try to put Trinity just four points behind. Shortly afterwards, he was tripped by Salford centre Stuart Littler who was immediately sent off by referee Russell Smith.

Five minutes later, near to his own line and immediately in front of the Wakefield spectators, Goulding intercepted a Wakefield pass and began to gallop the length of the field in what looked like a carbon copy of Littler's earlier interception try at the start of the second half. But, as Wakefield hearts sank, Goulding was brought back by the referee for deliberate offside and shown the yellow card. As he left the field, possibly as a consequence of some verbal exchange, he threw the ball at Trinity's Justin Brooker and the two were joined in exchanging punches by several other players. At the end of the melée, Goulding left the field but was shortly afterwards ordered back on by Mr. Smith to receive the red card along with Brooker.

With Salford down to 11 men and Trinity to 12, Neil Law took advantage of the extra man to score his second try. After Pearson added the goal the visitors were in front for the first time since early in the first half. With the scoreboard indicating that Huddersfield had indeed beaten London, as the clock ticked away, Wakefield fans had a further scare when at 26-24 Salford's Francis Maloney had a try disallowed. The home side had substitute Warren Stevens placed on report following a tackle on Waisale Sovatabua and Pearson added a further two points to Trinity's lead from the resulting penalty.

With only seconds left, Salford's Graham Holroyd was given the red card for tripping Trinity hooker David March who almost immediately then crossed his opponents line for an injury time try. Trinity had won 32-24 and their fans went wild. Huddersfield, not Wakefield, would go down.

Coach John Harbin's after-match media comments had by now become legendary and occasionally the subject of wrath in the Trinity boardroom and reports to Rugby League headquarters. He summarised the match by saying there had been " plenty of traffic coming past me in the dug-out all afternoon". Referring to Trinity's traumatic ups and downs he said "Wasn't there a movie called the *Never Ending Story*? Either that or *Monty Python's Flying Circus*."

The Fox brothers with David Hinchliffe MP at the Wakefield launch of *Rugby's Class War* in October 2000. Left to right: Neil Fox, Don Fox, David Hinchliffe MP and Peter Fox. (Photo: Julia Hinchliffe)

That match frankly had almost everything a contest can offer. The precipice of relegation was avoided by the narrowest of escapes in a game which had some fine competitive football but also explosions of indiscipline which are an inevitable part of the drama of a great contact sport.

The celebrations that day were on a par with anything I recall in over 40 years of watching the team. They were not just about avoiding relegation at the very last minute but also about coming through one of the most traumatic periods in the club's history when its very existence had at times seemed threatened.

I was behind the posts – this time at the St Michael's Lane end of Headingley – for another dramatic match in 1979. It is often said that there is nothing worse than losing in the semi-final of the Challenge Cup when you have been so near to a Wembley appearance. But with seconds to go Wakefield Trinity were losing 7-6 against St Helens with a place in the final against Widnes at stake.

Play was at the opposite end of the field with Trinity in possession and the Wakefield fans fearing the final whistle at any moment. As the referee looked at his watch, Trinity stand-off David Topliss broke the Saints defence and parted to former England Rugby Union centre Keith Smith. After making good ground on the South Stand side of the field, Smith fed winger Andy Fletcher who raced to score the match-winning try in front of the ecstatic Wakefield ranks, Trinity winning 9-7. Sadly, there was to be no

Cup Final victory for the team that season, my second visit to Wembley with Wakefield Trinity.

Wembley

My first trip to the great old stadium had been over a decade earlier when Wakefield Trinity faced the old enemy, Leeds, in the 1968 Cup Final. I must have played in or watched thousands of games of Rugby League but this is the match which I and numerous other Trinity fans of that era will never forget. It is a game which features time and again on our television screens, with arguably the most memorable Rugby League moment of all time.

I saw every game of that 1968 cup run, paying my one - and so far only - visit to Craven Park, Barrow, in the first round. I recall sleeping in the back of a van in Ambleside churchyard between watching Castleford play at Whitehaven on the Saturday and seeing Trinity beat Salford at the Willows the following day in one of the early Sunday matches.

I was playing regular amateur Rugby League at the time and, along with a number of my fellow players, planned to hire a minibus to travel to London and back on the day of the final. A complication arose because none of those able to drive was over 21 and we had the greatest difficulty obtaining insurance which had to be arranged by the hirers. Eventually, we found one company prepared to take us on and were all set for the London trip.

On the Thursday before Cup Final day, we learned that our insurance company had gone bust and as a consequence had to abandon our original plans and try and get down by train. The only way of avoiding the overnight stay we couldn't afford was by travelling overnight because all the Saturday Wembley specials were by then booked up.

We departed from Wakefield's Westgate Station around midnight, jammed into one of the old-style carriages with bench seats, no corridors and passenger access through the outside doors opening on either side of the train. Those who got any sleep had bagged the luggage racks. The rest of us passed a seemingly endless journey in an excited banter of anticipation of a great match.

Trinity by then had reached a period of uncertainty. By that I mean that the inevitable successes of the early 1960s had passed. While legends of the great days, such as Harold Poynton and Neil Fox, were still around, the stalwarts of the Trinity pack of the 1960, 1962 and 1963 Cup victories had largely called it a day. We could no longer always bank on the result going our way.

We had, however, clinched the Championship the week before, after beating Wigan at Belle Vue in the semi-final 26-9 - Billy Boston's last match for the Pie Eaters - and Hull KR 17-10 in the final at Headingley. The down side was that our scoring machine - Neil Fox - had suffered a recurrence of a troublesome groin injury and was out of the Wembley side. Leeds had finished top of the league to land the League Leadership Trophy and were probably that season's most consistent side. The neutrals were suggesting they were a good bet to prevent Trinity winning the double.

Because my father suffered frequent periods of chronic illness when I was a child and, when he was working, always had to do Saturday morning overtime, I had to make do with seeing Trinity's earlier Wembley triumphs on television. 1968 was my first visit to Wembley and it is hard to describe the feeling of climbing the steps to emerge into the huge chasm of that great stadium for the first time.

Our position was on what was then the terraced standing area to the rear of the posts at the end of the stadium from which the teams enter. Stood slightly to the Royal Box side of the posts, we were to have probably one of the best views of the controversial incident which was to markedly influence the game's result.

Our journey to Wembley and walk from the station to the stadium had taken place in glorious sunshine but, an hour before kick-off, as we stood in our places for the pre-match entertainment, the heavens opened with rain, the like of which I have never seen before or since. There were arguments at the match (and very many since) that, with much of the pitch under a sheet of water, the 1968 final should never have gone ahead. But there was obviously too much at stake for referee Hebblethwaite to call it off and neither he, nor anyone else, could have anticipated the further huge thunderstorm which again flooded the pitch during the half-time interval.

The players slid and skidded around in huge swathes of water with scoring chances arising primarily from their opponents' inevitable mistakes. Leeds were leading 4-2 from penalties midway through the first half, when Trinity's Don Fox put an astute kick through to the Leeds left-hand touchline. Leeds winger, John Atkinson, tried to keep the ball in play but slipped and Wakefield's Ken Hirst was there to kick ahead and score. A Fox conversion made it 7-4 to Trinity at half-time.

The further torrential rain made handling next to impossible and, in the second half, Don Fox's kicking continued to trouble Leeds. With just over 10 minutes to go Trinity looked to be in the driving seat, but what happened next is rarely shown when the 1968 final is featured on television. Leeds kicked into the Wakefield half and Ken Hirst, like Atkinson earlier, slipped while trying to cover the ball. Wakefield's problems were added to when their other winger, Ken Batty, also slipped, injuring himself some 15 yards out from the Trinity posts.

But Wakefield still appeared to have the situation covered when Atkinson and Gert Coetzer, Trinity's South African centre, skidded along apparently steadying themselves by holding on to each other. As they tangoed towards the line, Wakefield centre Ian Brooke collected the ball cleanly and set off to clear his line.

When the referee blew and pointed to beneath the Wakefield posts the Trinity fans and neutrals at the players' entrance end of the stadium, behind the posts, all assumed he had blown for a drop-out, adjudging Brooke to have touched the ball down behind his own line. To the utter amazement of both sets of players and, I suspect, the vast majority of spectators, it became clear that Mr. Hebblethwaite had awarded a penalty try to Leeds, determining that Coetzer had obstructed Atkinson and prevented him scoring.

The *Yorkshire Post* journalist, the late Roger Cross, an award-winning writer (but Wakefield lad, it has to be admitted), subsequently initiated the Hebblethwaite Myopia Award for the most questionable refereeing decisions and there can have been few more questionable than this. For an obstruction try to be awarded the rules required (then and now) the referee to be satisfied that the player allegedly impeded would otherwise have scored. With the exception of Mr Hebblethwaite, it was obvious to all present that, regardless of the tangle between Atkinson and Coetzer, Wakefield's Brooke clearly had the ball covered.

The 'obstruction' try - awarded under the posts - was converted with no difficulty by Leeds full-back Bev Risman taking them 9-7 in front. He added another 2 points moments later when, after Trinity knocked on at a play the ball near their opponents line, they were penalised for a tackling offence after Leeds had taken advantage and moved into the attack.

At 11-7 to Leeds, with 2 minutes to go, the outlook seemed bleak for Trinity as their scrum-half Ray Owen placed the ball on the centre spot to re-start the game. Many millions have seen these last moments on endless television re-runs and it is unfortunate that the true context of the earlier controversial try rarely, if ever, features. In particular, it is a pity that the crucial role of Don Fox at that last kick-off is also so often missed.

Owen geared up to drive the ball to the opposite side of the field from the Royal Box where the Leeds forwards gathered in the hope of retaining possession to the final whistle. But Fox took Leeds by surprise by taking the kick-off himself and booting the ball behind the Leeds defenders on the other side of the field. On the Wakefield right wing Ken Hirst followed through as quick as a flash and, kicking the loose ball over the soaking pitch, beat the Leeds defenders to dive on the ball behind their posts. 11-10 to the Loiners with the conversion to be taken in front of the posts immediately before the final whistle.

The rest is history and one of the most talked about moments in British sport. What went wrong has been the subject of endless debates ever since, with a variety of theories put forward. Some, who were at the Leeds end of the stadium swear a gust of wind blew a small wave of water which moved the ball just as Don Fox took the kick. Some suggest he slipped in the run up, others that the cotton wool packing his boot toe-cap had become soaked in the terrible conditions.

The great pity of it all is that Fox - voted the winner of the Lance Todd Trophy man-of-the-match before the missed kick - is remembered for the failed conversion rather than for a quite masterful display in the most difficult conditions imaginable. He was one of the finest players I ever saw perform.

Many years later Bev Risman told me that at the time of the 1968 final his wife Ann was expecting their first child and a week overdue. She insisted on being at Wembley, but was only allowed at the match on condition of being chaperoned by a doctor. It must have been quite a feat to get through that amazing match in her condition. With Neil Fox injured, Bev was chosen to lead the Great Britain Lions to Australia immediately after the final. And Risman junior finally arrived, none-the-worse for the foetal experience, on the following Saturday while Dad was thousands of miles away Down Under.

Undoubtedly, one of the greatest memories of my sporting life was being at Wembley for that remarkable 'watersplash final'.

Lord Doug Hoyle:
9 Wolves - by a whisker

In writing a chapter for this book I could not decide which of the many matches I have watched over the past 21 years I should write about.

Would it be a game featuring the skill and finesse of Jonathan Davies or the silky play and match winning abilities of Alfie Langer or any of the other giants who have worn Warrington colours over this period?

In the end, it was none of these but a game in the current 2002 season which has been a roller coaster and a nightmare for Warrington Wolves. This once proud club which has never played in any other than the top league throughout its history was facing the threat of relegation to the Northern Ford Premiership.

All through the 2002 season our future status was in doubt along with fellow strugglers Salford, Wakefield and Halifax.

As the current chairman of Warrington Wolves, I have a special interest and responsibility as we are hoping to move into a new stadium in 18 months time.

The game against Leeds Rhinos was a very important one for the Wolves. On level points with Salford and Wakefield at the bottom of the table we had not gained a win since beating Wakefield at home on 9 June. Indeed until the Leeds match we had only won 3 matches all season. These were the opening game against Halifax, a surprising victory at Hull on 5 May and Wakefield in June.

To say that it had been frustrating and disappointing season for Warrington's loyal and suffering fans is the understatement of the year. They arrived at Headingley for the Thursday evening game against Leeds Rhinos knowing they needed a win but expecting nothing against a Leeds side containing stars such as Francis Cummings, Keith Senior, Kevin Sinfield and Tonie Carroll to mention just a few, and heading comfortably for a play-off place.

For myself I arrived at Leeds after a terrible and debilitating car journey from London of four and three quarter hours and only reached Headingley 10 minutes before the kick-off at 8pm.

As always Headingley presented an ideal setting, despite the rain with the famous cricket ground on one side which itself has been the scene of many famous test matches and is the home of Yorkshire County Cricket Club. The rugby ground as always had a large crowd for a Thursday evening, of just over 9,000. Leeds are one of the best supported clubs in

Super League. Their supporters are partisan, but very knowledgeable about their favourite sport Rugby League.

Warrington Wolves had Lee Penny back in the team. Lee or 'Jimmy' as he is better known in Rugby League circles was in his benefit year but had been troubled by injury. Included also were Warrington's recent £40,000 signings from Wakefield, Nathan Wood, a very experienced No. 7 and Ben Westwood, a highly promising young centre of whom great things are expected in the future. Also playing in the Wolves' line-up was Danny Halliwell on loan from Halifax. Halliwell has been unable to get in the first team with the Yorkshire club, but was proving to be a valuable addition to the Warrington ranks.

However, the player who would be of most interest to the Yorkshire crowd was Sid Domic, one of Warrington's overseas signings from Penrith Panthers. Comparatively unknown, he had been a revelation and in his own words was playing the best rugby of his career.

However, Warrington approached the match very much as the underdogs. Although Headingley has always been a ground on which we have fared well and have given Leeds a close game over the last few seasons, the disparity between the teams with Leeds near the top and Warrington languishing at the bottom tipped the prospects for the game very much in Leeds's favour.

The game started as per the form book. Mark Calderwood scored for Leeds within three minutes, Kevin Sinfield kicking the goal and Leeds were demonstrating their powerful play and making it look easy, After 12 minutes, their dangerous winger Karl Pratt went over the line for a further try. This time Sinfield missed the kick.

Despite a Warrington reply after 15 minutes from Ben Westwood plus a successful conversation from Lee Briers, Leeds replied with a further try from Andy Hay on 21 minutes which was once more converted by Kevin Sinfield. Worse was to follow. Leeds went further ahead on the 29th minute when Chev Walker finished off a length of the field move leaving Warrington's defence in disarray. The reliable boot of Kevin Sinfield made 4 points into 6.

At this stage after 29 minutes Leeds were winning 22-6 and coasting to an easy victory. Nothing in Warrington's display so far pointed to the dramatic turn round in their fortunes that was to occur in the second half. It had been a mediocre performance. So far the match had followed the familiar pattern that Warrington supporters had become accustomed to in their club's worst season for years.

This was for the team to fall behind early in the game, in this case after three minutes, with a Calderwood converted try. Then, as in previous games, the team would rally taking the match to their opponents only to fall further behind. Usually they would then manage a reply, but their opponents were by half-time in firm control with a substantial lead which could become a rout in the second half.

Although Warrington did, in this game, reply with a further Ben Westwood try in the 30th minute, when he got on the end of a Lee Briers grubber kick, which was converted by Briers, it did not do a lot to lift the spirits of the drenched Warrington supporters. Briers had a hand in creating both tries as well as converting them.

Nothing in the first half, however, prepared the crowd for the Warrington fight back or for the dramatic and staring role that Lee Briers would play.

Half-time

At half-time the home side led by 22-10 and nothing could lift the spirits of the Warringtonians in the crowd. It seemed very likely that Leeds who had put in a professional performance, despite the rain and a pitch that was wet on top, which led to errors, would build on the substantial lead that they had.

This however, did not come about. For 20 minutes the score remained at 22-12 to Leeds Rhinos. It was not until the 68th minute that Lee Briers produced another of his long kicks which was seized upon by Danny Halliwell who twisted and turned his way over the line to score. Unfortunately this time Briers' kick let him down, but the score had become 22-16 with Warrington playing the better rugby in the second half. It presented them with a chance of victory.

Even better was to materialise from Warrington's point of view. Although the play swung from end to end it was Warrington who obtained the next points.

The Halliwell try was the beginning of Warrington's spree of 11 points in the last 12 minutes of the game. Super Sid Domic was to show how invaluable he is to the Warrington side. On the 71st minute he twisted first this way then that to force his way over the Leeds try line to bring the score to 22-20. The tension throughout the ground built up as Lee Briers prepared to attempt the conversation. Every Warrington fan was hoping he would succeed while every Leeds supporter was willing him to miss. In what seemed an age Briers placed the ball on the spot and re-adjusted it. The ball moved again only to be re-adjusted and finally the kick 'sweet as a nut' sailed between the posts.

This was a match for brave hearts certainly not for poltroons. The game itself swung from end to end with fast running as both sides were trying to get into the all important position to attempt a drop goal which would give them a win and two points in the league.

The atmosphere was unbearable. Both sides desperately needed the points: Leeds to strengthen their quest for a play-off place, Warrington to put points between themselves and the bottom clubs Wakefield and Salford.

The tension got to both sets of players. Mistakes were made when they seemed to get into a scoring position. This was not surprising given the nailbiting situation. Despite the watery conditions no one was leaving the stadium - all eyes were glued to the pitch watching a match which had turned from being a stroll for Leeds to one that hinged on one side or the other getting near enough to their opponents' posts and creating space for their kicker to attempt a drop goal.

Minutes had been slipping away, indeed when Warrington drew level only nine minutes remained. 71 became 72, then 73, then 74, then 75, then 76, then 77, then 78 and still the scores were level. Was the result going to be a draw with both sides sharing the spoils?

78 minutes became 79 and no one could bear to look when Lee Briers obtained the ball for Warrington just over the half way line. Despite the difficult conditions he decided to attempt a drop goal. He swung back his foot the ball swirled high in the air and soared towards the Leeds sticks. Would it go over the posts? All eyes turned to the flight of the ball. In what seemed an interminable age the ball remained in the air until finally it went between the posts to give Warrington a drop goal and a deserved victory.

What had been a mediocre match had turned into a breathtaking climax, one that would be remembered by people, particularly Warrington supporters, for a long time.

This was the Lee Briers' match. He had a hand in all the tries, missed only one difficult kick, and produced a match winning final kick that was worthy of any block busting epic.

Was this going to be the turning point in what has been an extremely disappointing season for Warrington? Unfortunately the jury is still out, The team's form is still indifferent and our future in Super League with 5 matches remaining in doubt At this stage we are on equal points with Wakefield. one point above bottom club Salford and two points behind Halifax,

However, this was Dave Plange's finest hour as Warrington's coach. Unfortunately due to the teams indifferent form he has since left his position but nothing can take away from him the stirring performance that brought

Warrington back from the jaws of defeat to victory courtesy of Lee Briers' boot.

Headingley was a great victory. A late season revival meant that Warrington Wolves would continue to play in Super League in 2003.

Leeds Rhinos: Cummins, Calderwood, C. Walker, Senior, Pratt, Sinfield, Sheridan, Adamson, Diskin, McDermott, Hay, Carroll, Vowles. Subs: Ward, Poching, B. Walker, Burrow.
Scorers: Tries: Calderwood, Pratt, Hay, C. Walker. Goals: Sinfield (3)
Warrington Wolves: Penny, Alstead, Burns, Westwood, Halliwell, Briers, N. Wood, Laughton, Clarke, Hilton, Fozzard, Marquet, Domic. Subs: P. Wood, Guisset, Crouthers, Noone.
Scorers: Tries: Westwood (2), Halliwell, Domic. Goals: Briers (3). Drop-goal: Briers.

Above: Hull FC versus Hull KR at Wembley - 1980 Challenge Cup Final. Sammy Lloyd tackling Len Casey (Photo: Courtesy Robert Gate)
Below: Hull KR supporters' banner recalls their win, on display at Workington in April 2000. (Photo: Peter Lush)

Lindsay Hoyle MP: Being Chorley's chair

It now seems a long time since I first became involved with Chorley, back in 1988. I was the young, thrusting opposition spokesman for Economic Development and Tourism at Chorley Borough Council, and Springfield Borough Rugby League Club came to pay me a visit. They were struggling at that point. In fact, they were only a stone's throw from going out of existence; and I decided to support them. Sport can do so much for a town, and I was deeply proud to see the former Springfield team move to Chorley and cap a successful first season as Chorley Borough they became the youngest member of the Rugby Football League.

From that moment on, Chorley was an adventure, a labour of love, and I do know I made some great and lasting friends in rugby, both on and off the field. I particularly remember Carl Briscoe, who played out his career at Chorley. From the very beginning, he was one of our best players, as well as one of the most dependable and popular. He was always great fun, too, so long as you didn't forgot he was utterly driven by money. You never knew where you were with Carl, not until you had sorted out every single one of his idiosyncratic contractual requirements. He would even hold out for a free pair of bootlaces to be provided for every game. And then - after his contract was signed - he would be 100 per cent loyal to you. Carl still takes a keen interest in the game and carefully watches his son, Sean, at Wigan.

There was also Aaron Whittaker, a Kiwi who originally came to us from Hull KR. Hull had too many overseas players at the time, and they suggested that we take him on board - and what a tremendous asset he was. From the very start, we could all see he had talent, but he just grew and grew in stature, eventually going on to play the game at the very highest level. He turned out for the Australian Super League side Penrith, as well as touring Great Britain as a Kiwi international. It was great to meet up with him and talk about the old days - and we still keep an eye on each other's careers (I even got a letter from him when I became an MP).

It wasn't ever about making money. All the Chorley directors were rugby fans, men who wanted to give something back to the game they loved. Between us we ran the club and I was appointed chairman. We did have a respectable amount of success in our first season, and we played some wonderful cup games. In particular after the first season at Chorley, efforts were made to establish the club as Trafford Borough instead of Chorley. This caused months of upheaval but eventually the Chorley club remained intact, and Trafford emerged as a separate club. Ironically, soon after, the

Lancashire Cup draw paired Chorley against Trafford. It is difficult to tell whether more blood was spilt in the boardroom between directors or on the field on that day, but eventually Chorley won by a single point leaving a very sweet taste at our Victory Park for directors, players and fans alike.

In following years other cup games included matches against Wigan, Warrington and Castleford. But more importantly to me, we travelled to a lot of grounds that are no longer with us. It was the twilight years of semi-professional Rugby League, and although I'm probably not allowed - as a New Labour MP - to feel any kind of nostalgia about it, I still do.

The turning point, sadly, came in 1992. The rugby club had shared Chorley's football club's ground since its birth; but that year saw the arrival of new managers at the football club, and they did not want the Rugby League club around. This was a backward move, in my view. It was clear, even then, that the future lay in multipurpose grounds. Chorley Borough moved to Horwich. Crowds and performances started to deteriorate.

It was around that time, too, that we first started hearing rumours that Rupert Murdoch had his sights set on Rugby League. Australian Rugby League was about to enter into one of its bitterest and most bloody battles off the field and it was only a matter of time before this had an impact in Britain. I dare say some shake-up was inevitable, and in many ways badly needed. Football was undergoing a renaissance in the wake of the Taylor report and the BSkyB cash bonanza, while Wigan were in danger of monopolising Rugby League. Few clubs had been able to follow in their trailblazing footsteps after the 1985 Challenge Cup, and there was a very real risk that the game would lose its spark and excitement.

Super League

But for all that, I believe that Super League was not what Rugby League needed. The project grew out of Murdoch's attempts to wrest control of the Australian League competition from rival TV mogul Kerry Packer: and time and again it fundamentally misunderstood the nature of the game. No-one wanted to watch a supposedly Parisian club dominated by Australians; still less did anyone want to see Warrington and Widnes clumsily merged to form a team called 'Cheshire', as was suggested in 1995-6. And when clubs around me started to support the Super League plans I couldn't help thinking of turkeys voting for Christmas. Rugby League needed to put its house in order. It didn't need to sell its soul.

A lot of pressure was put on us down at Chorley. We were told that we had to take the Murdoch shilling, that it was the only way for the game to

Lindsay Hoyle MP (Photo: Courtesy Lindsay Hoyle)

grow, that we were obstructing the progress of the game - and so on, and so on, ad nauseum. I simply didn't believe it. The scheme evidently had all kinds of advantages for bigger clubs, but I couldn't accept it because Chorley, and clubs like it, might be kicked out of the Rugby League family forever. Naturally, this view didn't fit in with the plans of the Rugby League board.

They were set on claiming that their members unanimously wanted the Super League deal, and leaked as much to the press. Nevertheless, on the day the proposals were put to the clubs, Chorley voted against. I was the representative for Chorley at that momentous meeting at Central Park. To this day I'm glad we voted the way we did.

Why do I say that? There are a number of reasons. Certainly our recalcitrance helped bring about some frenetic renegotiation. Money was eventually set aside for the game's future grassroots development, and Chorley received some of that money. I don't believe that you should ever give in easily when people try to force your hand. I'm very pleased we didn't at Chorley. Also, the original proposals called for a reduction in the size of the leagues which amounted to the bottom three teams of division two being kicked out. This obviously affected Chorley because we were near the bottom of the league and while we were extremely unlucky to finish in this position (due to an amazing result for Highfield over Barrow at Barrow) the club did suffer as a consequence.

It's not as if I foresaw what would happen with Super League from the start. All the same, I did suspect that Murdoch's plans were both half-baked and ill-advised. So much cash went into the game as a result of the Sky television deal - yet what have we seen in the way of long-lasting improvement?

Money has been frittered away on players' salaries. Second-rate overseas players, who should never have been seen in Super League, have been bought and sold as if there was no tomorrow (surely it is time that the number of overseas players was reduced, from five to three or two). Stadiums have scarcely improved, and I do think the first years of Super League will go down in Rugby League history as the wasted years. A golden opportunity was thrown away.

Above all, I thought then, and still do, that there was a very real danger of the game we love being lost. If there is a way forward for Rugby League, it lies in working together. Super League seemed to forget that at first. They pitched club against club, chairman against chairman, player against player. I think back now to men like Denis Ramsdale. An ex-Wigan player, his career had been cut short by injury when he came to us at Chorley.

He contributed an extraordinary amount to our team as a player, and is still with us to this day, as chief executive. For Denis and for any true fan of rugby, this game is about community. For similar reasons, I won't forget Bob Eccles, an ex-Great Britain international who chose to finish his career at Chorley, first as a player, then as a coach. Anyone who knows Rugby League well will recall his days at Warrington; it truly was an honour to be associated with someone of his immense stature. As a prop forward, he was ahead of his time: for here was a fast, agile, athletic player, at a time when most props were huge, awkward hulks of men, leaning on one another all the time. Bob signalled the start of a new breed. But more than anything else, he was a great ambassador to the game. The family spirit of rugby ran through his blood: he respected the game, was always willing to promote the game, and he was always willing to spend time with other people to try and strengthen the game.

That's why the loss of the old cup competitions, with the coming of Super League, has been so tragic. The days of the Lancashire Cup, the Regal Trophy, the Silk Cut Challenge Cup (played at the end of the year), and the Premiership play-offs, really were the halcyon days of Rugby League. No matter how strong Wigan were, you couldn't ever say for sure who would win: and unless we try to strengthen the game at all levels - without exception - we won't be able to have those days back again. We won't manage to broaden the game's appeal. We won't generate enough passion to get in the new fans whom we so badly need. I wonder whether the game will get the sort of corporate sponsorship we're looking for. Though we are a small club here at Chorley, we invariably have great sponsorship, starting off with Multipart, then British Aerospace, then Scottish and Newcastle, and so forth. I think that's because companies believe in Rugby League, first and foremost, as a community sport. It is imperative that we recognise that.

The 2002 one-off test against Australia proved that there is a huge gap in the standard of rugby played here in Britain compared to Australia. Super League has not been the answer to everything and we have to learn the lessons from recent experiences. The reorganisation of the Rugby Football League and the appointment of a new board of directors has to be a good thing and I believe it is time for everyone to work together in order to advance the game.

As for Chorley they are still playing at Victory Park where the adventure started all those years ago. Despite having an extremely good season when playing as Lancashire Lynx, I do not believe that Chorley have really recovered from the period where Super League was established. However, gradually the team is improving and I hope that Chorley will go from strength to strength, working with the local community and extending its base of loyal support.

After being selected to fight the parliamentary seat of Chorley for the 1997 general election I realised that, given my workload, my days as chairman of Chorley Rugby League Club could not last and I stood down.

However, the first thing I did when I became an MP was to join the All Party Rugby League Group, and I am never afraid to say that Rugby League is without doubt the greatest game in existence. This is because for my money, if you can get somebody - anybody - to watch three games of Rugby League, three weekends in a row, he or she will then be hooked on the game for life.

But the game needs strength in depth. I hope the Super League episode has taught us that lesson. It is all too easy to watch a club go by the wayside, as very nearly happened to Chorley, and once it's gone, it really has gone forever. It isn't good for local communities, and it isn't good for the spirit and health .of the game. Rugby League will only move on and fulfil all of its insatiable ambition by remembering its roots. Let's hope it happens.

Lord Geoffrey Lofthouse (boy on left in front of barrier) at what
may have been his first game at Featherstone
(Photo: Courtesy Lord Geoffrey Lofthouse)

Tony Cunningham MP at the Rugby League Fans' Petition presentation to
Parliament March 2002 (Photo: Peter Lush)

Peter Kilfoyle MP:
I'm sure I recognise that prop

The first time I arrived in Australia, in 1975, I must confess that I was abysmally ignorant of the country. I knew it was big, warm, and part of the Commonwealth. Indeed, I saw it as a sunnier version of Blighty where most things would be familiar, including its sports. As with most anticipations in life, I was to discover that my little knowledge was a truly dangerous thing. My culpable ignorance of the lucky country was truly sublime.

I had alighted upon the shores of Botany Bay with a one year contract to teach physical education. I assumed that I would be allocated to a country school, and convinced myself that I would be going into work each day on horseback. Instead, I was given a school in Liverpool, in the western suburbs of Sydney, in a neighbourhood inappropriately named the Green Valley. From Liverpool, in Britain, to Liverpool in Australia was not just a huge step in time and space, but also in culture.

I race ahead. The induction course was designed to prepare us for the culture shock of life down under, and was successful in parts. Yet it was a social event, a freebie, which was to give me the first major indication of this exotic world quite unique in its approach to life, including sport.

My wife and I were given complimentary tickets to a function at the Canterbury-Bankstown Rugby League club. The tickets, although free to us, had a face value of $1 per head. Apparently, this was a requirement under state laws, although I was baffled by the economics of the evening, given what went with the ticket. Firstly, there were two happy hours, during which one paid half the price of a single drink, while receiving the double. Secondly, the bearer of the ticket was entitled to a meal in the club restaurant on the night - for free. Finally, there was entertainment laid on, in the club's concert room.

Memories came flooding back as I looked back on cold Saturdays spent watching Liverpool City play when I was a lad. I even reflected on prized visits to Knowsley Road or Central Park, Naughton Park or Wilderspool - to see the greats of yesteryear like Billy Boston, Tom van Vollenhoven, Brian Bevan or Eric Ashton - or giants of the pack like the -Vinty Karalius -"Wild Bull of the Pampas", Alan Prescott or Abe Terry.

Such thoughts also evoked long-suppressed recollections of the bland flavours of allegedly meat pies or doubtful cups of ersatz tea. If there was entertainment, it consisted of the characters on the pitch and the wags on the terraces. Of course, there were social offerings for adults at the clubs, usually consisting of a resident trio, with a stand-up comedian.

Canterbury-Bankstown was on a different plane. A huge, purpose-built club, with sumptuous furnishings, and a variety of bars. The food was of a quality and a quantity much appreciated by an aspiring *bon viveur* like myself. Drinks were cheap without halving the price and doubling the quantity. As for the entertainment, it was the legendary Dionne Warwick, then still at the height of her international celebrity.

The key to how such clubs could offer such fare and diversion lay all around me. There were literally hundreds of 'pokies' - one armed bandits - banked along every wall, with eager customers plugging in their coins in contented monotony hour after hour.

The attendants working at the club - on the door, monitoring the rooms within, supervising the machines - included playing staff under contract to the club. It could not have been further away from Rugby League as I had known it. It was professional in every sense, well organised and well funded, explaining and ensuring the success of Australian Rugby League.

It was not as if there was no competition. Others codes flourished then, and continue to do so. Admittedly, there were, and remain, regional variations; but League prospered alongside Rugby Union, association football, and that great Antipodean mystery, Australian Rules, a game which defies description by a mere Pom.

I was to discover during my seven years in Australia that there were, of course, similarities to the sporting scene in the Britain, especially with Rugby League, as well as differences. The code remained a premier choice for working class Aussies, as Rugby Union reflected an Australian class divide similar to our own.

This was hardly surprising because Rugby Union derived its strength from the private school system within Australia. Blue collar workers took great pride in their roots, and the Rugby League sides which championed their communities. As the former Labor Prime Minister of Australia, Paul Keating, used to say: "You can take the boy out of Bankstown, but you cannot take Bankstown out of the boy" - referring, of course, to himself and his own community roots.

It was one of the reasons that the Australians took imported Poms like Tommy Bishop to their hearts. They could identify with Tommy, and he with them. They admired not just his playing skills, but his courage - the diminutive Tommy would stand up to anyone. In so doing, he epitomised the little "battler" so beloved of the Australian working class psyche.

So, my introduction to Australia was bound up with my introduction to Australian Rugby League. With hindsight, that was entirely consistent with understanding how Australians tick. I was to be taken by the Australian obsession with sport, and with Rugby League in particular. By the time I moved north to Brisbane - another Rugby League redoubt - a night at Lang Park watching the footie, eating pie and peas, and swilling down a tinnie of 4X was as natural as could be.

Pub-based Rugby League

Yet there was another facet of League of which I was unaware until after I had gone from Sydney to live in Brisbane. I refer to the flourishing amateur competitions, run in the wider Brisbane area. Being from Liverpool, I was aware of the massive Sunday league competitions run for the benefit of amateur football. It was not until I arrived in Queensland that I experienced a parallel development of pub-based Rugby League.

Now I should point out that as a young man, I played Rugby Union competitively, due to an 'advantaged' education. I watched League, but had no real skills in the game. Besides, as time wore on, opportunities to play anything competitively became more infrequent, due to pressures of family and work. I had happily settled for the spectator role, when one of those rare opportunities which a wise man would have passed up on, came my way.

A friend of mine was still a keen amateur Rugby League player. His best days behind him, he enjoyed his weekend outing for the Balmoral pub, a dockers' watering hole. Inviting me down for a drink, to my shock and horror, he volunteered me to play in their next game. I felt shoe-horned into agreeing. Bizarrely, the team was sponsored by the Painters and Dockers Union, and for the reasons which I could not quite divine, I ended up with a union membership card for their union. A strange outcome for a teacher.

On the fateful day, we travelled to the north side of Brisbane for the game, against the Redcliffe Hotel. My trepidation was diluted by the repeated assertions by my team-mates that it would be a nice weekend run out. As a former hooker, I was put in the front row as a prop and I assumed that I could coast through without too much mishap, and all would be well.

Imagine my horror, therefore, when onto the pitch lumbered the intimidating bulk of the boss of the Redcliffe Hotel for a little exercise. It was Artie Beetson, the then recently retired former captain of Australia and doyen of prop forwards - and he was propping against me! Apparently, he liked the odd fling at his old game. The sudden onset of panic was only just controllable as I looked for a way out.

I could not fake injury before the game began, and desperately tried to think my way through my plight. Before I could assemble my thoughts, the game was on, and due to a combination of my reluctance to get close to the ball and my colleagues lack of success in moving it, I avoided contact with the opposition until the first scrum.

As we went down - not too far, as Artie was over 19 stone, and didn't deign to really bend - I felt a low yield atomic device explode in my ribs. I exaggerate - it was a friendly tickle from Artie. To emphasise the message, a side swipe of the head of Artie as the scrum broke up left me feeling a tad giddy.

Not all of the longshoremen in the side could transfer their handling skills from the dockside to the rugby pitch, and we had repeated breakdowns of play, and repeated scrums. These were not the relatively skilled, if tough, manoeuvres of the professionals - more like repeated bar room brawls. It was no longer fanciful to fake injury - I was injured, bruised and bloodied!

Discretion being the better part of valour, I gave in to the mounting fear that Artie might do something really serious and I went off injured within 15 minutes of the kick-off, with no intention of returning. Ironically, within five minutes, Artie went off, having had his fun for the day. He probably repaired to his hotel to cool off with several kegs of lager.

But what of me? I scampered away before the 'game' was finished, never to attempt to play a game of either rugby code again. I still wake at nights with that image of a gargantuan Artie Beetson looking at me with entirely deserved contempt. Still, 1 am not without some fond memories of Rugby League. Not of playing, but of the equanimity with which grown men can knock the hell out of each other in the name of the sport of Rugby League, without any lasting rancour. That is as true of the game in Australia as it is in England. Just to prove my point, I have no grudges against Artie. That is, as long as he stays in Australia, while I can still cower in England.

Artie Beetson (Photo: Courtesy Robert Gate)

Lord Geoffrey Lofthouse:
Not just a sport - a way of life

Featherstone Rovers Rugby League Football Club was created in 1902 as a junior side and through its success from 1919 to 1921 an application was made for admission to the Northern Rugby League which was successful and the Club attained senior status for the 1921-22 season.

Not being born at the time - this came three years later - I was, of course, not aware of the influence that it would have on the whole of my life and still continues to today.

Little was I aware when my mother's brother, my Uncle Jim, took me to see Featherstone Rovers play in about 1931, and neither, I suspect, was he, what effect his actions would have on the remainder of my life. Since that date, my passion for this great game has never waned. Since that time, the game of Rugby League football has been my passion and has filled a major leisure and recreation part of my life. I am sure my Uncle, long-since dead, could never have appreciated what a fulfilment he gave to my life when he introduced me to the game.

Apart from supporting my beloved Featherstone Rovers, I was to enjoy 20 years of my life playing the game and the friends and, indeed, the comradeship made in those years has remained with me throughout my life. The Featherstone Rovers club exists in the small mining town of Featherstone with a population of about 15,000 people. The town's economy for most of my life was mainly supported by the local coal mine and the hard working miners whose main sporting activity and interest was Featherstone Rovers.

Like many communities in the 1930s and 1940s and into the 1950s, transport to the town from others areas was limited. There were very few people who owned cars and apart from an occasional visit to the adjacent towns of Pontefract and Castleford, they were confined to Featherstone for their recreation and while there were the working men's clubs, one cinema and two dance halls, this was the limit. However, this was in many ways an advantage. It created a family community where everyone knew each other.

Rugby League was a major part of the town's life. The game was played in local schools. There was the usual rivalry between schools, both in Featherstone and surrounding areas. The greatest ambition of boys of my generation was to play in the school team. It meant you were really someone at school if you played in the Rugby League team.

I recall with pleasure that when the school team was playing away at another school on Saturday morning, the players were allowed to take the school shirt home after school on Friday. I recall you would put the shirt over your shoulders and tie the arms around your neck. This indicated to the town that you were in the team. You were really somebody among your peers.

This meant much more to most of the boys than any academic achievement because most of the boys considered that whatever they achieved in that field would be somewhat irrelevant to most of them because they knew at the age of 14 years, like myself, they would be going down the coal mine. This resulted in their ambitions to succeed as a Rugby League player and indeed play for the Rovers. If this was achieved they would work in the pits and would also earn a small amount of money over and above their wages from the colliery playing for the Rovers. This, in some small way, made them the aristocrats of Featherstone but their main satisfaction was the pride they had in playing for their home town club.

In the early days of my association with the club the results on the field were mostly unsuccessful because they were competing with clubs from larger towns whose finances were far greater than theirs and who could offer to pay higher wages and consequently could attract star players.

Yorkshire Cup Final

When I was aged 14 years I first saw Featherstone Rovers win a trophy in the 1939-40 season. This was during the Second World War. They played Wakefield Trinity in the Yorkshire Cup Final at Odsal Stadium, Bradford and Rovers won, 12-9. This was a real tonic for the town, the whole family of Featherstone celebrated.

After the war, when people in Featherstone started to become more affluent, the colliery was working to capacity, women had gone out to work in the war years and continued to do so. The club became more financially secure although it was never wealthy.

Through the amateur game the club began to produce a host of star players and also attracted a few seasoned internationals. The first break into the big time was in 1952 when they reached the Rugby League Challenge Cup Final played at Wembley, but unfortunately lost to Workington Town 18-10. As many as 15,000 of Featherstone's population attended. All shops were closed, the local colliery recorded record production levels during the cup run.

This started a period when the club, between 1959 to 1993, appeared in 18 finals including the Yorkshire Cup and the Rugby League Challenge Cup. Considering this small town of 15,000 people could produce a team that could play in the Challenge Cup Final at Wembley five times and win on three occasions, plus winning the Rugby League First Division Championship in 1976-77, mostly by players born in Featherstone and the surrounding districts.

I have always taken great pride that my nephew Vince Farrar captained the Rovers in their Championship season and that both Vince and another nephew Barry Hollis, played in the 1972-73 Challenge Cup Final when they beat Bradford Northern 33-14.

I also had the very proud moment when the Rovers won the cup at Wembley in 1966-67. I was Mayor of Pontefract that year. My very good friend Malcolm Dixon, a great forward, was captain on that occasion. What a thrill he gave me when he turned up at the Mayor-making ceremony and presented me with the Rugby League Challenge Cup. Rugby League certainly put Featherstone on the map.

During the period I have referred to, the club produced many great players, too many to mention achieved the game's highest honours, including county, international, test match and selection as members of touring teams. I remember when a player was selected for a honour, how proud the town was. I also remember when I first went to Parliament, some Members of Parliament from the South would often say, "Where do you come from?" and when I replied, "Featherstone", they would immediately say, "Featherstone, the rugby town?" They had not forgotten the Wembley appearances.

I know what the team meant to the local community. I know there are many other rugby league communities like Featherstone whose clubs I believe have been dealt a near fatal blow by the News International deal, backed by media giant Rupert Murdoch, which introduced Super League.

The great thrill of small clubs like Featherstone in the period I have referred to was playing top successful teams and occasionally beating them. Star players would be spread more evenly across the league and in general would remain at one club. Of course there were occasions when the smaller clubs had to sell their star players to maintain financial viability and this is how Featherstone survived because they could always produce players to take their place.

For all Rugby League clubs there was always a burning desire to play in the cup final at Wembley. The BBC had always, through the radio and later television, broadcast the final which over the years became a national occasion greatly appreciated by the southerners, not least the police, who were grateful for the good behaviour of the northern Rugby League visitors.

I was always very appreciative of the coverage the BBC gave the game, not least the finals because it gave many passionate supporters of the game, who were unable to travel through age or infirmity, many of them miners suffering from chest diseases, the chance to hear or see the game.

In these circumstances, I was greatly concerned when an advisory group was set up by the Department of Culture, Media and Sport to consider which sporting occasions should be protected for terrestrial television, thus stopping those events from being taken over by the likes of Sky Television. If this was allowed to happen, it could deny many Rugby League supporters the opportunity of seeing the final in the comfort of their own homes because they could not afford Sky television.

To my great concern when the group which was chaired by my colleague Lord Gordon of Strathblane, produced their report, they recommended that although they recognised that this event had great significance in certain parts of the country, they did not feel either that it possessed great national reasons for the whole of the UK or that it could be said to be a more meaningful event than, say, the international matches of the Great Britain team. They recommended that the Rugby Football League should be at liberty to sell the rights to televise the Challenge Cup Final to either terrestrial or subscription broadcasters and they saw no reason to hamper its' ability to do this by listing the event.

Accordingly, they did not recommend that the Rugby League Challenge Cup Final should be added to the proscribed list. I was very upset. I took the view that the Advisory Group, which had among its members such distinguished sports personalities as Jack Charlton, member of the England 1966 World Cup winning team and Steve Cram, the international athlete, had missed the point. It appeared to me they had made the judgement on a commercial basis without recognising the social consequences in the Rugby League communities of the game not being on terrestrial television.

Defending the Challenge Cup

I was so concerned I corresponded with Chris Smith, the then Secretary of State at the Department of Heritage, requesting him not to accept the recommendations and I made an application for a debate in the House of Lords to enable me to present my case. I was successful in obtaining a debate opposing the contents of the report which I am delighted to say was successful and the Rugby League Challenge Cup Final has remained on

BBC television. I have always felt honoured that I was in a privileged position to put the case for Rugby League.

Following my speech I corresponded and had meetings with Chris Smith, then the Secretary of State, Department of Heritage in which I emphasised to him the importance of the Rugby League Challenge Cup Final being available for all television viewers and drew his attention to the contents of my speech. I was delighted at a later date that the Secretary of State announced that he would not accept the recommendations of the Advisory Group, and had decided that the Rugby League Challenge Cup Final should be protected from the commercial market and that it should remain on terrestrial television.

I can understand my opponents' argument on a financial basis and I recognise the need for clubs to be financially viable. However, that should not be the only criterion and supporters of the game should also be given serious consideration.

I take great satisfaction that my arguments seem to have won the day and the many Rugby League supporters, many of them elderly, unable to travel to the Challenge Cup Final, and unable to afford subscription television, will have been able to continue to watch the final on the BBC.

It was a great shock to the Rugby League world when it was announced in 1995 that the Rugby Football League had accepted a deal with News International. The deal was for the rights for the Murdoch organisation to televise Rugby League for a payment of £87 million.

This caused great concern because the announcement was sudden and there had been no pre-warnings that such an offer had been made. One of the main concerns was that some of the old established clubs would have to merge to meet the conditions of the agreement.

It was in fact recommended that Wakefield, Featherstone and Castleford should merge and form a team called 'Calder'. Considering the healthy rivalry between these clubs covering a period approaching a century, it is not difficult to understand the reaction of the supporters. They were concerned that many of the clubs' chairmen had been bounced into the decision through their own club's financial difficulties and I suppose the chairmen understandably took the view that this vast amount of money could solve the games financial problems.

Regrettably, this does not appear to have been the case. Most of the clubs do not appear to be any stronger financially than prior to the Murdoch deal. I find it regrettable that some of the money did not find its way down to the grass roots. I always believed that the Murdoch money should have been shared out more equally, say 10 per cent into an essential fund and 10 per cent to BARLA for the amateur game. The Rugby Football League would still have been left with £60 million. Some of this should have been set aside for improvement of facilities at the clubs and whilst I must stress I do not begrudge players their rightful rewards, I do not think it has been for the benefit of the game that most of the Murdoch millions has been spent on players' contracts.

I believe the pride of local players from smaller clubs has been diluted by the Super League riches. It certainly appears to me that the emphasis is on the elite super twelve with the rest begging for crumbs from the rich man's table. Only time will tell us if the rest of the game outside the Super League can exist on the crumbs.

The British Amateur Rugby League Association, known world-wide as BARLA, has been one of the sporting success stories of modem times. The Association was formed in Huddersfield in 1973 as a breakaway from the Rugby Football League, which at that time was controlled by 30 professional clubs, with the amateurs having no vote or say in their own destiny. The sport was seen then, by many, to be in serious decline with little more than 150 amateur teams, with youth rugby being down to as little as 30 sides. Such was the stark reality of the situation.

When you consider 29 years later these figures have increased to well over 1,000 teams of which more than half were in the crucial area of youth and junior rugby, BARLA's 29 years of continuous growth is a truly remarkable record. What other sport or business could boast such an impressive growth record? And I pay tribute to all who have voluntarily worked so hard to achieve this for little reward apart from their love of the game and their interest in youth and young children.

There is a future for BARLA, while recognising we have to strive for excellence in the professional game, this must never be at the expense of the grass roots game. However, in 2002 Sport England has adopted a pro-active approach to rationalise sports administration. The aim is one sport, one governing body and therefore as a recipient of exchequer funding and lottery sports funding, Rugby League administration, encapsulated by the British Amateur Rugby League Association, the Rugby Football League and the Rugby League Policy Board is faced with inevitable change.

Despite real concerns evidenced by BARLA, arising prior to the new administration led by Executive Chairman Richard Lewis, that the RFL had effectively discarded the partnership agreement binding the Rugby League Policy Board, it is obvious that the sport must move on.

It appears the Rugby League Policy Board in the absence of meaningful power and authority has effectively served its purpose having allowed the sport to speak and act as one and in the process access a wealth of public funded opportunities hitherto beyond the grasp of Rugby League.

The RFL, by creating a new Board encompassing the Executive Chairman Richard Lewis, a finance director and three non-executive directors, not attached to clubs, has introduced a neutral leadership for the game and has paved the way for the RFL to adopt the governance of the game and not the demands of the Sport England. It appears this neutrality means BARLA will be unable to have dedicated representation on the RFL Board, a condition I understand applies to Super League, the Association of Premiership Clubs and all other Rugby League agencies.

But it is essential that BARLA's identity is preserved and the Association continues to represent the grassroots of the game. However, BARLA would no longer carry the status of a governing body per se and the ability to directly access exchequer funding.

I believe BARLA's democratic structure should remain and the association's general assembly, the board of management and its sub-committees should continue to contribute to the policy-making process. It will also be essential for BARLA to have representation on the RFL's operational board that will be responsible for the day to day running of the RFL and policy creation.

BARLA would effectively be reliant on the RFL for funding however there must be guarantees that will ensure the financial viability of BARLA in particular the association's access to exchequer funding via the RFL.

I understand that change is never easy. However I believe the work of the Rugby League Policy Board has created a platform for a better future that can only effectively be realised by a single governing body. To realise that future and the true potential of Rugby League, BARLA must take a leap of faith, one that will preserve and enhance the Association's pivotal role in the game's development under the auspices of an independent RFL Board.

I am optimistic for the future of the game if all sections work together to advance what I personally believe is the best game in the world. I hope greed of the few will not devour the weaker sections of the game.

1967 Challenge Cup Final: Barrow versus Featherstone Rovers. A triumph for Lord Lofthouse's team who won 17-12. (Photo: Courtesy Robert Gate)

Hull versus Halifax in Super League August 2000.
The modernised Threepenny Stand is in the background.
(Photo: Peter Lush)

Alice Mahon MP: Fax and figures

Halifax is a Rugby League town. We do have a football team, but the majority of the people follow Rugby League. The team was well supported at the old Thrum Hall ground, but I feel that support has fallen since the changes in the game prompted by Rupert Murdoch and the summer season.

I was brought up on Rugby League. The conversation in our house would be what was happening at Thrum Hall, or what was happening in cricket – village, county and test – depending on the season. My father was a very keen cricketer, but the real sporting love of his life was Rugby League and Thrum Hall. Of course we used to discuss the Labour Party as well – my parents were lifelong socialists.

Some of my feminist friends pull a face when they find out I am interested in rugby. They have an image of rugby from Rugby Union. But my image of rugby is Rugby League, which I have followed since I was a child. My mother was very keen, and as many little girls as little boys would attend matches at Thrum Hall. But my father was the big influence on me and gave me my love of the game.

People don't realise that hooliganism is anathema to Rugby League. It is a completely different culture to football. In the 1950s and 1960s one policeman was enough for Thrum Hall, and he would usually watch the match.

Odsal 1954

One of my first memories of a Halifax big occasion is the 1949 Challenge Cup Final, when we became the first team not to score at Wembley. But the one that really stands out is the 1954 Challenge Cup Final replay at Odsal. I remember going to the match, and there were about 120,000 people there. Thousands didn't pay – they climbed over the fence. I walked there and back. The roads were completely blocked, the whole of the Calder Valley. Every road from Warrington was full. There was huge enthusiasm for that match. I remember walking home from Odsal with my dad and my sister. We waited outside the pub while he stopped for a pint!

There was great excitement over that match, even though we didn't win. It is one of my abiding memories of Rugby League. The town was buzzing for weeks with the whole experience. Brian Bevan, the Australian winger played for Warrington in the final. I remember the talk on Sundays in the Working Mens' Club about him.

I remember when Johnny Freeman signed for Halifax from Welsh Rugby Union. We had had Maori players before, but he was one of the first players of Afro-Caribbean descent at the club. He was a friend of my father's sister and was very popular in the town. Years later my eldest son was friends with his daughter at school. My father had a pub at one time and the players would often come in. I remember Billy Boston coming in after one game.

Another great memory is the 1987 Challenge Cup Final at Wembley against St Helens. I was standing for the Halifax seat and went to Wembley as the prospective parliamentary candidate. I was wearing my blue and white scarf and my rosette. I was going to have a photo taken with Neil Kinnock, the Labour Party leader. He met us, with all his aides, and we had the photo taken. It was a happy one with me wearing blue and white, and it created the best promotional leaflet we ever did. Halifax had won the cup, so we headed it "Backing the Winner". In Siddal, Ovenden and Pellon – all Labour and Rugby League areas – people displayed that leaflet in their windows. And on the loudspeakers during the election, we adapted the Halifax chant "'Ali, 'Ali, 'Ali Halifax" – 'Ali' is close to my name.

For the 1987 Challenge Cup Final I was on the terracing, and we won the cup – just. John Pendlebury saved the match for us in the last minute, knocking the ball out of Mark Elia, the Saints' centre's hand as he was about to score. The celebrations were fantastic – no one wanted to go home. The Mayor organised a reception for the team on the Town Hall balcony and thousands of people came. I've still got that rosette and scarf.

For the 1988 final, I was back at Wembley, but in the royal box! I had won the seat in 1987 from the Tories, one of the few gains we made that year. I was a left-wing MP, and there I was in the royal box with the mayor, an old-fashioned Conservative called Wilf Sharpe. He was there with his consort. But that day there were no differences between us – we were both very excited and supporting Halifax. It was a lovely occasion although we lost to Wigan. Neil Kinnock was there again. But it wasn't quite as good as 1987 or 1954 – they were special.

Rugby League is well represented in Parliament. People like David Hinchliffe and Ian McCartney have worked very hard for the game. Many of us were not happy with the changes when Super League came in. We felt that part of our culture had been taken over by a big corporation. Somehow part of the heart of the game had gone. But Maurice Lindsay and his supporters were determined to see this through. I remember the speech that

Odsal 1954: The Halifax versus Warrington Challenge Cup Final Replay
(Photo: Courtesy Robert Gate)

Ian McCartney made that year at the Rugby League Parliamentary Group annual dinner. He summed up our concerns very well.

I still go to the games when I can, and I still enjoy it. I don't mind the razzmatazz and the Blue Sox name, although my husband Tony, who is a Rugby League fanatic, doesn't like the new name. And I don't mind playing at The Shay. It's in a great setting – the Halifax hills, Piece Hall nearby, stone buildings. When it is finished it will be a nice stadium. It will link with the other facilities nearby – Spring Hall stadium, which needs a new track, and the bowling greens. It will be a superb sports facility for the town.

One match I went to recently was against the Bradford Bulls. There were lots of children there having a good time. And I like the players mixing with the supporters in the bar after the game. Robbie Paul was there, talking to everyone. That's one of the great things about Rugby League – everyone mixing.

The amateur game is important as well and has a big tradition in the town. Recently Tony and I went to watch Siddal in a cup tie. It was raining all the time, and it was a very hard match.

The Blue Sox are involved in the local community as well. One of the schools in my constituency, The Ridings, had a lot of problems, which have now been resolved. I went to watch the Northern Broadsides Theatre Company, an amateur actors group, perform there. Three or four of the Blue Sox players were there as well. They also help coach local amateur and youth sides. The game is played in the schools and children are encouraged to play Rugby League.

For the first few months of the 1997 Labour Government I was Chris Smith's Parliamentary Private Secretary when he was Minister for Culture, Sport and the Media. I went to Wembley to the Charity Shield match between Chelsea and Manchester United in his place. We were thinking of going to Lords, because women weren't allowed in the Pavilion then and we wanted to challenge this. I have a lot of admiration for Chris Smith, I think he did many good things for sport and the arts, and it's unfair that he's been blamed for the problems with Wembley. My role there ended when I voted against the government in December 1997 over cuts in child benefit and was sacked!

My husband Tony is passionate about Rugby League. If we are on holiday or away on Parliamentary business and the Blue Sox are playing he will ring home to find out the result and details of the match. My oldest son Chris is a barrister and lives in London. He loves the game and goes to watch the London Broncos when he can. But he is a Halifax supporter – I can buy him anything from the Blue Sox as a present.

I enjoy watching football as well. My grandchildren enjoy it – the seven-year-old supports the Blue Sox, and then Arsenal or Manchester United – he can't decide! But I was raised on Rugby League and that is the sport I enjoy most.

Sir Brian Mawhinney MP:
14 Taking comfort from the game

My friend, John, arrived at our north London home about 11.00am to have his customary cup of coffee before we set off for Wembley. It was Saturday, 3 May 1997 and we were going to watch Bradford play St Helens in the Silk Cup Challenge Cup Final. It was the 100th anniversary of the first final in 1897, which also involved St Helens.

John and I have been friends for over 25 years. A Yorkshireman, and passionate supporter of Halifax, it was he who introduced me to Rugby League. For a number of years we had been privileged to watch Challenge Cup Finals, in latter years as guests of the Rugby League. On this particular Saturday we were again the Rugby League's guests.

We had debated whether or not to go. Neither of us had had any sleep on the Thursday night. During part of it we had driven, as the dawn broke, from Peterborough to London so that I could be present for the change of government.

Friday 2 May had started with me being a senior member of the governing Conservative Cabinet, re-elected to the House of Commons, where I had served for 18 years. It finished, after an afternoon audience with Her Majesty, with me being an opposition MP - for the first time.

We decided to go to the game. Life properly had to move on. Anyway watching a good game of rugby would be pleasant and a helpful distraction.

After we had sat down for lunch I noticed that the new Deputy Prime Minister, John Prescott MP, was the guest of honour. Should I or should I not? I should. Getting up from the table I approached John. Was it my imagination or did conversation quieten in the room? I congratulated him on his victory and wished him well in his new responsibilities. He quickly translated cautious surprise into a gracious response. I returned to my seat and general conversation resumed.

And the game? St Helens won, again. Rather against the odds we had seen them beat Bradford the previous year. This year Bradford wanted revenge - badly. Their pre-eminent position in the league was impressive. But would their mental strength equal their physical? Eventually the answer was "no".

It is always difficult to separate out the details of one particular game but some memories of that one linger. St Helens and Bradford fans mingled comfortably and without incident on the way to Wembley. There was plenty of the usual good natured singing, exchanging of slogans and emptying of beer cans but none of the tension which, occasionally, these can cause among a minority of football fans.

Robbie Paul played like gifted footballers do. As the Bulls' captain he urged his men on and it was only after he damaged his foot in the second half - subsequently revealed to be a broken bone - that the Saints scored their winning tries. If my memory is correct the post game pundits also heaped praise on Bradford's Steve McNamara for his kicking and neat passing as well as his place kicking.

Bobbie Goulding was outstanding. In the previous year's final his soaring kicks had undermined Bradford. This year his kicking drove the team down the touchlines with the same impressive result.

But he was not the only St Helens star. Tommy Martyn played brilliantly. He scored two tries and made two others. None of us was surprised when he won the Lance Todd Trophy as man-of-the-match.

After 20 minutes Bradford led 10-4. Eight minutes later the sides were level and St Helens never looked back. Indeed it was only a Bradford try and conversion two minutes from the end that made the result more respectable.

32-22 for St Helens felt about right. Bradford's Australian coach, Matthew Elliott, admitted after the match that his team had failed to take advantage of their opportunities. St Helens took more of theirs.

I am no Rugby League expert. I enjoy watching the game because it is straightforward and uncomplicated, tough, skilful and frequently faster than you might think. A real battle of wills, as well as skills.

That day we saw an excellent example of the game at its best. All of us who were privileged to be there enjoyed an excellent afternoon's sport. The reputation of both clubs and their supporters was enhanced.

John Prescott presented the Cup to St Helens. Both subsequently went on to other newsworthy achievements.

As for the Bulls, although they lost that day in May 1997, they are still a force in the land. Personally I find that strangely comforting...

Bradford Bulls: Spruce, Ekoku, Peacock, Loughlin, Cook, Bradley, Paul, McDermott, Lowes, Reihana, Nickle, Dwyer, McNamara. Subs: Tomlinson, Medley, Knox & Calland.
Tries: Peacock, Loughlin, Lowes, Tomlinson. Goals: McNamara (3).
St Helens: Prescott, Arnold, Haigh, Newlove, Sullivan, Martyn, Goulding, Perelini, Cunningham, O'Neill, Joynt, McVeigh, Hammond. Subs: Pickavance, Matautia, Northey, Morley.
Tries: Martyn (2), Sullivan, Joynt, Hammond. Goals: Goulding (6).

Ian McCartney MP: Murrayfield to Murrayfield via Central Park, Wigan

It's 1962 and I've just received a letter that's about to change my life forever. It simply tells me, 11 plus 'pass on appeal'! A place at the prestigious Lenzie Academy. Short trousers, little caps and a blazer to boot. I can cope with this but I can't cope with playing rugby instead of football. I want to cry and cry.

The great day came late for me because I had spent the summer and the autumn in hospital recovering from a bout of chronic osteomylitis. I arrived at the Academy sporting a large stooky (plaster) and a pair of nifty crutches, which were constantly stolen from me.

Day two. My first PE session and my life began to change. Because of my illness I had little confidence either in my academic or physical abilities and was an angry and frustrated boy because of it. As I stood propped up on my crutches watching fellow pupils put on their shorts and gutties (plimsolls) the man they called 'The Bull' strode up to me, looked me up and down, put his hand on my shoulder and said "McCartney, we are not only going to make you walk again, we're going to get you running and playing rugby".

This was the first person outside of my family who had given me any hope that I could beat the chronic osteomylitis and do the things my mates were doing. Billy Williamson, affectionately nicknamed 'The Bull' had been a famous post-war centre-forward playing for Glasgow Rangers, an icon of his time, built like Billy Boston he was held in awe, tough but fair. The strange thing was how could such a famous footballer teach at a school that had banned the round ball in favour of the oval ball?

The Bull worked with wee Johnny Magee who enthusiastically took on the job of getting me fit and generally running the anger and frustration out of me. Within weeks we had discarded the crutches, got rid of the stooky and were running barefoot in the snow to "build up my character". I had chilblains bigger than tennis balls but I loved it. Academia was out the window and sport took over my life.

The Bull and wee Johnny placed me in Lennox House and I was quickly promoted to the cross country team and the Rugby Union team, although swimming was becoming a bit of a disaster. I just couldn't get the breathing right and tended to sink to the bottom without a trace! My dad got me a rubber tyre from the local garage but it was so big I slipped through the middle straight to the bottom of the pool. I was clearly never going to be a "Thorpedo"!

Forty years on and I can just fit into my dad's old car tyre. Forty years of training on pies and pints and, with the onset of New Labour, a few scoops of Cabernet Sauvignon.

Rugby first time

Back to 1962. I got my hands on a rugby ball for the first time. Wee Johnny was a brilliant coach. He wanted rugby to be played with the ball in hand, fast, creative and above all, he wanted you to play for the jersey. He wanted you to spill your guts for the team and he was a great motivator.

Rugby and running became my way of life and the politics came along with them. Every Saturday morning a group of working class lads who all played football but who had passed the infamous 11 Plus pulled on their Lenzie jerseys and wore them with pride. We played the cream of Scotland's private schools and beat them all. We were undefeated but such was the elitism and snobbery of the Scottish Rugby Union none of the Lenzie Academy team were ever picked for school honours. We had some great players. I was in awe of some of my schoolmates, the power of their speed and handling was before their time. Everyone would have made great Rugby League players but we were banned from playing it.

Early morning cross-country running. Saturday morning playing rugby. Saturday afternoon going with dad to watch Kirkintilloch Rob Roy. The Rabs were at the time the premier junior football club in Scotland, hosting a range of stars that went on to become famous professionals. When dad couldn't take me I went on the team bus and always sat, if I could, with Martin Ferguson, brother of Alex Ferguson. Even back then I was trying to rub shoulders with the famous.

Having been won over to playing Rugby Union, I started to enjoy playing it more than football and this coincided with the Eddie Waring days on the BBC. We didn't have a telly and so I watched BBC at my mate's house. There was a Rugby League sevens tournament at Wigan's Central Park and I was immediately drawn to Billy Boston. I think it was because physically he was a close resemblance to 'The Bull' although Billy was taller. I was hooked. At the age of 13 I became an avid fan of Rugby League and Wigan was in my blood, forever - but more of this later.

Wee Johnny and 'The Bull' started to take us to Murrayfield to watch Scotland as part of team building exercises. They had a block booking for the schoolboys' stand which was situated around the pitch side at the old

Murrayfield ground with fabulous views of the action, which was important for me at the time as I was probably the smallest 13-year-old playing rugby in Scotland.

I did say 'The Bull' was a bit of a disciplinarian, firm but fair. I was to find out all about his firmness following one particular sojourn to Murrayfield. It was a rare occasion, the mind's a bit hazy but I believe it was a victory against France. As the merry whistleblower put his hands in the air to signal the end and Scotland's triumph, a whippet aka one Ian McCartney set across the field at right angles followed by hundreds of spotty teenagers from the schoolboys' stand - it was like a scene from *Braveheart* and little did I know what was to happen on the Monday morning when I arrived for my PE class.

Standing silently, looking menacingly at me were wee Johnny and 'The Bull'. My classmates were all put in line standing as if they were part of the Black Watch Battalion on guard at Edinburgh Castle. Then, the fateful words were spoken, "McCartney, come to the front", "McCartney, give me your gutty". "Which one, sir?" "You choose, and bend over." "Why, sir? Why?" "You've disgraced the school, it was Murrayfield you were at, lad, not a riot on Glasgow Green".

Yes, 'The Bull' could be tough. I think I still have the marks today. I was simply a boy before my time. A few years later it became the norm for youngsters to run on the pitch at the end of internationals.

When I left Lenzie aged 15, my last recollection was leaving the PE hall with a pair of rugby boots whistling past my ears, thrown by one of the most hated teachers in the school, a man called 'The Bullet'. I thought his teaching technique was simple - belt the living daylights out of you! I used to dream about getting him on the blind side of the scrum and stamping him on his head and loosening a few teeth.

When I left Lenzie in 1966 little did I know how big an influence 'The Bull' and wee Johnny was to be three decades later. The taught me how to play rugby, but unwittingly they had introduced me to the politics of rugby and my true love, Rugby League.

Wigan

In 1973, my journey back to Murrayfield began. There is a by-election in the Westhoughton Constituency on the doorstep of Wigan and a young Roger Stott won a landslide victory for Labour and he advertised for an Agent. I apply. The chance to go to Central Park at last. Good interview, but its not to be and I'm not offered the job and my journey back to Murrayfield via Wigan has been put on hold until early in 1979

I received a telephone call from Roger Stott at my home in Dover and he asked me if I would come to live in Wigan and reorganise his political office and local party. Wigan, the world's capital of Rugby League - there could only be one answer. "Yesssssssssssssssss."

Many people in politics in the north-west have believed that I came to Wigan because I had ambitions to become an MP. I can reveal nothing was further from my mind - it was the rugby, Rugby League. Over the next few years, working with Roger Stott, I had a really nice sideline going. Roger started campaigning in Parliament and with the support of BARLA to expose the discrimination and bigotry that Rugby Union had systematically practised against our beloved sport.

It was too late for me to play the game, but I certainly wanted my son, Hugh, to do so and so it wasn't just a matter of watching Rugby League at Central Park. Hugh joined Ince St Williams Amateur Rugby League club and spent many happy hours on a Sunday morning visiting St Helens, Widnes, Swinton, Warrington and other exotic places, playing his heart out, living his dream of one day being Henderson Gill.

From the 1979-80 season until the 1988-89 season, Hugh and I went to every single Wigan game, home and away, it was our time together. We learnt much about the Rugby League heartland, its communities, and its traditions, its essential honesty and class-consciousness. It was a period of change not just for Rugby League, but also a social and economic upheaval with a loss of much of our heartlands, industry and infrastructure being lost. It wasn't just hard on the field, off the field it was even harder and courage had to be displayed. Rugby League was an essential and critical element in the maintenance of our beleaguered mining and industrial communities.

Hugh learnt not just rugby, but politics and I became deeply politicised about rugby's own class war.

In 1984, I took another step on the road back to Murrayfield, I was a patient in Leigh Infirmary. Problems, which had dogged me from the days of chronic osteomylitis, had returned. A major operation on my left femur and knee was required. My leg pinned and painful, was about to suffer a rather pleasant shock. A delegation of Labour Party members from the Makerfield constituency asked to see me outside visiting hours and told me that in my absence there had been a little meeting of 'friends' who believed that the sitting Member of Parliament, Michael Maguire, a life-long St Helens Rugby League supporter, was likely to be challenged. My friends were concerned that any challenge would be divisive when the Labour Party nationally had not yet recovered from its worst ever election defeat. They felt that I was the one person that could unite the local party if a selection battle was joined. I had in fact already decided to leave my Labour Party employment and seek a university place to train as a barrister. However, the prospect of living with three young children on an MP's wage sounded a lot more pleasant than struggling on a student's grant. The rest is history as far as this chapter of my life is concerned. A Wigan fan had defeated a Saints fan.

In 1986, I was invited as a parliamentary candidate to visit the Parliamentary Labour Party offices in the House of Commons and on that day I met two people who became lifelong friends. Dawn Primarolo and one David Hinchliffe. I knew Dawn by reputation, she had been titled 'Red Dawn' and when we were elected in 1987 we were listed in *The Times* as two of Labour's most dangerous left wing candidates. I had met David briefly at a local government conference in Nottingham and he had the day before been served with a writ by his own Council Leader in Wakefield banning him from entering the Town Hall. I thought, here's a rebel with a cause and what a cause it was to be.

Labour whips

We were elected to parliament and by sheer coincidence, the Labour whips office allocated David Hinchliffe and me desks next to each other. What made it even more ironic was that the Labour whip who allocated the desks was a Welsh Rugby Union fanatic who believed that Rugby Leaguers were the scum of the earth. The sporting war to end all sporting wars was about to begin. David and I believed the formation of an All Party Parliamentary Rugby League Group was essential if we were going to end Union's discrimination against League. A campaign plan had to be organised. The politics of ideas and the politics of organisation were to be brought together and on 10 February 1988 the Group was formed.

The Parliamentary Rugby League Group was, in my view, to become one the great teams in the history of Rugby League. And when, in late August 1995, exactly 99 years and 364 days from the beginning of Rugby Union's class war against League, the blazer brigade and the 'old farts' club had to own up to their bigotry, their elitism and their hypocrisy and put their game on an honest and equal footing with Rugby League. We had won the war not only for the right to be on the pitch, but to be treated with dignity and respect and with growing acknowledgement of the sporting prowess and athleticism that Rugby League brings to the world of sport.

David's book *Rugby's Class War* sets out the game plan and the strategy of our Rugby League Group. Much change has taken place and continues to take place between Rugby League and Rugby Union such as the sharing of facilities, the sharing of players, playing in each other's tournaments, working together to develop the talents of both young boys and girls and respecting each other but still having a healthy rivalry. In years to come there may be further changes. Each game has got outstanding athletes and talent. Each game has got a myriad of disciplines which are so essential in helping young people build up their self-awareness, their personal skills, their fitness and health and both can evoke and put on huge sporting spectacles at both national and international levels.

Return to Murrayfield

My journey to Murrayfield started in 1962 and it took me 40 years almost to the day to return to Murrayfield via Wembley, the House of Commons and Central Park. My wife Ann and I, were so proud as we watched the Saints and the Warriors walk out on the hallowed turf of Murrayfield. The people of Edinburgh have taken Rugby League fans to their hearts. Rugby League is now being played across Scotland and there's a Scottish international Rugby League team I can support. No longer are young boys like me being banned from playing Rugby League. In Easterhouse, one of the most deprived areas in the east end of Glasgow, the young people living there have been introduced to Rugby League. They have a team to play for and to support.

The 2002 Murrayfield final was a classic Saints and Wigan encounter with Wigan coming out top. But the icing on top of my personal journey back to Murrayfield was yet to come. Dave Whelan, the present day owner of Wigan Warriors, invited me to the dressing room after the final to share with my team their moment of unadulterated joy at beating our auld enemy. The team had hatched an evil plan and I was to be the victim of six bottles of champagne being sprayed across my torso and brand new suit. For a moment I thought about mimicking the voice of 'The Bull', Billy Williamson and saying: "It's Murrayfield, lads, not the victory podium at the British Grand Prix, My name's McCartney, not Schumacher." But, what the hell, why not champagne, 40 years is a long time, it was a long journey? I had made it back but not unscathed.

As the stadium lay still and quiet and I licked the last of the champagne droplets from my suit lapel, I thought about that little boy running like a whippet across the hallowed turf, I just wished the impossible that the little boy for a few moments could have been my beloved Hugh. Tragically, Hugh died before our journey was complete but it was still a journey I was proud to have taken.

2002 Challenge Cup Final: St Helens 12 Wigan Warriors 21

St Helens: Wellens, Albert, Gleeson, Newlove, Stewart, Martyn, Long, Britt, Cunningham, Shiels, Joynt, Jonkers, Sculthorpe. Subs: Ward, Stankevitch, Hoppe, Higham.
Tries: Albert, Gleeson, Sculthorpe.

Wigan Warriors: Radlinski, Dallas, Connolly, Ainscough, Johnson, O'Neill, Lam, O'Connor, Newton, C. Smith, Cassidy, Furner, Farrell. Subs: Bibey, Hodgson, M. Smith, Carney.
Tries: Dallas, Lam, Connolly. Goals: Farrell (4). Drop goal: Lam

Challenge Cup Finals: Top: Wembley 1997 Bradford Bulls versus St Helens. Below: Murrayfield 2002 (Photos: David Williams)

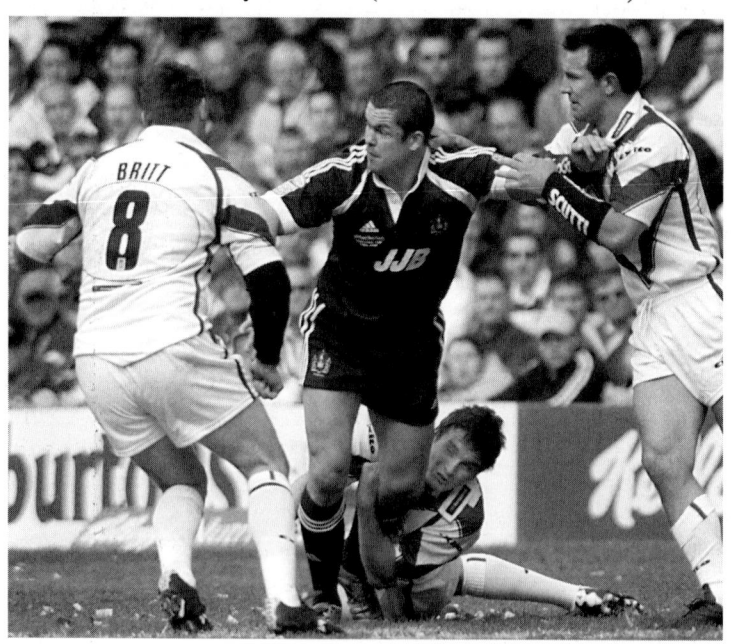

Kevin McNamara MP:
Two shares in Hull Kingston Rovers

My first memories of Rugby League are of occasionally watching Liverpool Stanley when I was at school in Liverpool. We played Rugby Union at school, and I still enjoy watching both codes. I didn't really get to know Rugby League properly until I went to University in Hull in 1952. I remember going with Roy Hattersley to watch Hull FC at The Boulevard. I saw the Drake twins play for Hull FC in the 1950s - powerhouses in the pack.

I stayed in Hull when I left university, got married and in 1966 was elected as an MP for North Hull. My wife is from Warrington, is a great Rugby League fan and recalls watching Brian Bevan playing for the Wire. We watched a lot of Rugby League in those days. My secretary was a great Rovers supporter, and she and her husband did a lot of work for the club on a voluntary basis. Rovers were also known as the "Irish" club in Hull, and the fact that they played in red and white all were reasons to support them.

Those were the heydays for Rugby League in Hull. Both teams were doing well, and they were great rivals. When they played each other there would be a huge crowd, some in red and white, some in black and white. Hull FC's support was from West Hull, and Rovers from East Hull. Rover's support then was based around the commercial docks, and Hull from the fish docks.

The late Norman Buchanan MP came from Glasgow to speak at a meeting for me. I took him to Hull Paragon station on the Saturday morning. It was a sea of red & white and black & white - everyone was travelling to a match outside the city, probably a semi-final. He was amazed that there were no police, mounted or on foot, and no dogs. Rugby League is a family game, genuinely the people's sport, there is no hooliganism.

At one time the family had five season tickets for Rovers. My sons played Rugby League themselves, before eventually becoming interested in other things. My second son, Kieran, played in the same youth team as Lee Crooks, with some very gifted players, and my other sons, Brendan and Edward, played as well. They played League at weekends, while playing Union at school during the week.

I find it difficult to go to matches now. From the time I was on the Front Bench, and the international travelling I do now, spending Sunday afternoons at home with my wife is precious for me. Nevertheless those were very happy days when we used to go to matches as a family. There was always a good atmosphere in the stand and the boardroom, and a good crowd.

The 'old' Craven Park ground was near the sea, and on cold winter afternoons, fog and mist would sweep over it. You would hear the cheers from the other side of the ground, and occasionally the players would emerge from the mist, but it didn't take away from the enjoyment. I remember France playing at Craven Park, and you could hear "Allez France" through the mist but I don't recall seeing the players. We had good times at the old ground. We could take the children. It was always a family game - wives were not left at home. The game was fierce and hard, but without the ruthless edge of some sport today. The players had tremendous skill and strength, which they still show today.

Kevin McNamara MP
(Photo: Courtesy Kevin McNamara MP)

I have two £1 shares in Rovers - I sold out to capitalism! But they are probably worth more than my other shares - the Hull Co-op and Kingston Communications.

The 1980 Cup Final, when the city's two teams met at Wembley, was a great occasion. Whatever happened, the cup was going to stay in Hull. Rovers won 10-5, and all the McNamara family were there - except father! I was on a plane above the Indian Ocean returning from parliamentary business in India. My wife took the children to the match. She told me about the seas of red and white and black and white scarves, people chatting before the match, all good natured. The family completed the final part of the journey by tube. Some started singing the "Red, Red Robin" Rovers' song. A lady on the train, completely dressed in Rovers' red, told them to behave, as they were "in London".

While the match was going on, Hull was deserted. There were no cars on the roads, the shops had no customers, and the shop assistants were watching the match on television. There were no burglaries while the match was going on, and at Wembley no arrests, except for a few people from Wakefield who were drunk.

Rovers have had some great players. Roger Millward, Clive Sullivan and George Fairbairn stand out. But for me Rugby League is about the whole team. We went to see the team, even though some brilliant players stood out. There was - and still is - strong tribal loyalty to the team.

Amateur Rugby League is strong in the city. West Hull and Hull Dockers have a fierce rivalry. Their matches draw good crowds, sometimes better than some of the professional clubs. Hull Dockers is a famous name, but there are few dockers in Hull now. The game is having a revival in the schools as well, although there is competition from Rugby Union, if only because it has larger teams.

Rivalry

The rivalry between the teams was present among my political colleagues. My agent for many years was Councillor George Templeman JP. He was a Hull FC supporter, and had played Union for the Navy. Even in the most tense election campaign, he would be at the match, while finding something else for me to do. Another close friend is the former Councillor Patrick Doyle, another Hull FC supporter. He has been a driving force behind the creation of the new stadium for Hull FC and the Hull City football team. The new stadium will be tremendous - a state-of-the-art venue in the heart of West Hull. As well as a new home for the two teams, they will have education and sports facilities for local people.

One of the best things in my time in this place [the House of Commons] has been the dedication of David Hinchliffe MP and Lord Lofthouse in working for the Rugby League. David has been a tower of strength for the game. Roger Stott, who for many years was the MP for Wigan, also worked hard on the game's behalf. He was a great Wigan supporter - his election address always had a photo of him at Central Park in front of one of the stands. Many of the Yorkshire and Lancashire MPs are supporters of the game.

When Selwyn Lloyd was the Speaker, until the early 1970s, he gave a reception for the clubs in the Challenge Cup Final in Speakers' House the day before the game. He had been Recorder in Wigan before entering parliament. I'm one of the last MPs who attended those receptions.

I spoke in the debate in the House of Commons at the time Super League was being proposed, regretting as I still do, the re-organisation of the game to please the Rupert Murdoch-owned media.

As in football, the difference between the big and smaller clubs has grown. Money is a big factor today and it is much harder for a smaller club to win promotion. The introduction of professionalism into Rugby Union will change both codes. I am not sure what the long term implications of this will be. I always opposed the apartheid between Union and League when Union was amateur, but there is a lot of money in the south east of England, and clubs there can attract players from the north and abroad. Small clubs in both codes will struggle.

Hull Kingston Rovers August 1959: Back: Holland, Jaques, Ackerley, Grice, Coulson, Taylor, Jenkin. Front: Paul, Kellett, Riley (capt), Key, Moat, Elliott. The team beat Warrington 18-13 at Craven Park. (Photo: Courtesy Robert Gate)

I still enjoy watching both codes, although I think the scrums in League could be improved. Sport has changed from my younger days. I have a cousin, Tony, who played professional football in the 1950s, for both Everton and Liverpool. He earned £15 to £20 a week - a good wage, probably twice the average, but nothing like today's players. But in Rugby League you can still meet the players in the bar after the game for a drink, and of course some of the old players run pubs in the town.

As a Hull MP for 36 years, and resident of the city for nearly 50 years, Rugby League has always been important to me and my constituents. In my original constituency, a majority were Hull FC supporters. My new constituency is more mixed. Both clubs have strong links with their local communities, and I am proud that a city of around a quarter of a million people has been able to sustain two very good Rugby League teams.

Lord Peter Smith: Murphy's magic day

For some clubs like Wigan, St Helens and Bradford, winning the Rugby League Challenge Cup seems to come easily. For the fans of other teams it is a dream they cling to, starting with great optimism as each cup season approaches. However, for most, the thrill of the final is something they will never experience. For fans of Leigh the dream became reality in 1971.

That year's Final was a traditional meaty Lancashire versus Yorkshire clash, but it is remembered, outside Leigh, as a notorious final because of the incident involving Sid Hynes, the Leeds captain. Since David beat Goliath the world has often cheered for the underdog. When Leigh made it to the 1971 final, their one and only Wembley appearance, they were expected to lose because most of the game's pundits, notably television's Eddie Waring, predicted an easy victory for the mighty Leeds. Leigh's player-coach Alex Murphy had other ideas, and, with odds at 15 to 1 against Leigh, as a natural gambler he placed his bets.

Rugby League is a sport that breeds characters, larger-than-life figures whose exploits continue to engage fans long after their playing days end. In the second half of the last century few exerted as much influence on the British game as Alex Murphy as both a player and a coach.

As a player he had vision, skill, physical presence and absolute self-confidence right from his explosion into the game as a teenager for St Helens. He is said to have demanded a transfer after a couple of games as a 16-year-old because he wanted a guaranteed first-team place. He went to Australasia as the youngest tourist on the legendary 1958 tour and played a full part in its success. He was one of the first code-crossers from League into Union during his national service with the RAF, helping them become the Inter-Service Champions.

Alex had strong views about his own worth and was impatient with the Victorian attitudes of administrators about a player's place in the game. Inevitably he clashed with the Saints' board, and the unlikely outcome of a long-running dispute about which position he should play was that he became coach for Leigh in 1967. Now lifelong Leigh fans like me began to expect things might start to happen.

Leigh are a small town club, proud to be one of the founder members of the Northern Union, indeed they were the first to be suspended by the Rugby Football Union for paying for "broken time". However, the club has suffered from periodic financial crises making it difficult to compete with Rugby League's bigger clubs. One of the game's hotbeds, Leigh has produced a stream of local talent but had not managed to win the cup since 1921, before the final was held at Wembley. Although usually hard to beat on their own 'midden', Leigh were not expected to win Rugby League's main prizes. They had managed occasional public relations coups like the signing of the sprinter McDonald Bailey who played only once, in a friendly that attracted 15,000 spectators, and scored a try. In 1961, when code-crossers went the other way, Leigh attracted the England Rugby Union star, Bev Risman, before he moved on to Leeds. Murphy's signing was different. Alex brought to Leigh not just his talent but also his ambition to succeed.

As coach Alex changed Leigh in three ways. Firstly he created an effective team by a combination of shrewd signings of older players, using his limited budget most effectively, and developing the talents of local youngsters. Among the most influential of the old pros he signed were Peter Smethurst, the Swinton butcher who had moved up from centre to loose-forward and was a good ball handler and formidable tackler; second- row forward the late Jeff Clarkson, who had barely started on his journey to become Britain's most travelled player (measured by number of clubs he played for); and Kevin Ashcroft, a Leigh-born hooker who was playing at Rochdale. Allegedly he had a clash with Murphy during a game and threats were made to continue the dispute after the match. However when Murphy turned up at Ashcroft's place of work next week it was to sign him not to fight him.

Secondly he got his players to play above themselves. Murphy's weapon was fear. Using language that would certainly be described as un-parliamentary, he made his players know what he expected from them and what would happen if he did not get it - most responded! One Leigh chairman commented, "Murphy really earned his money just before a match and at half time."

Finally he used his great tactical awareness of the game to exploit the rules that existed then. This was the era when sides surrendered possession after four tackles, reducing the opportunity to develop attacks. Murphy used a kicking game to establish territorial superiority and hoped to win subsequent scrums against the head (it did happen then) in the opponent's '25' to continue the attack. He also believed in the principle of not returning empty handed from an attack if possible by dropping goals, then worth two points. Indeed Murphy's tactics had helped persuade the game's administrators to make the game more open by reducing the value of a drop goal to a single point - but only after the end of the 1971 season. Being player-coach, Alex Murphy was not just giving the instructions but, as scrum-half, was in a pivotal position on the field to carry them out. No one would pretend that Alex Murphy's tactics produced attractive, open rugby to watch, but Alex cared about winning and, after their years among the game's also-rans, Leigh fans just loved it.

Leigh's great improvement

Murphy's influence was soon noticeable as the team's performances showed great improvement. They were serious challengers in the league and won the BBC2 Floodlit Trophy and the Lancashire Cup. But all Rugby League fans dream about winning the Rugby League Challenge Cup at Wembley. The 1971 campaign was to be the most memorable in Leigh's history.

The contrast between the two teams' progression to Wembley could not have been more marked. Leeds, playing their expansive style were comfortable winners in all their games. Leigh's progress was less convincing and included a narrow win over Huddersfield in the semi-final by 10-4 with all the points coming from goals. This helped establish Leeds as firm pre-match favourites.

Living in London

In 1971, I was living and working as a college lecturer in London so I could only see Leigh occasionally during the holidays or on television. On the day of the semi-final I was stuck in deepest Devon, accompanying a party of students on a pre-arranged trip. Only one of the mini-buses - not mine - had a radio and when some students told me Leigh had been defeated, the huge disappointment was something I had grown accustomed to over many years. It was several hours later that I discovered I had been hoaxed, but was too happy to care.

While living in London I always attended the Rugby League Cup Final with a few friends. Now I had to get tickets for more family and friends to see this historic game for Leigh fans. Around a dozen of us met up in the bar of Marylebone Station before journeying to Wembley by train. We were a quiet reflective bunch; a bit apprehensive about what the afternoon might bring after all those years of waiting and hoping. We wore our team favours discretely - except for my friend, the doctor. He had commissioned a special pair of clogs with Leigh motifs and unusually for the times, had acquired a club jersey. Dressed like that he stood out in central London!

We did not feel like drinking much and left the bar early to soak up the Wembley atmosphere on our big day. It looked like the whole of Leigh had come to town. Their ticket allocation had soon been snapped up and the fans had travelled by bus, coach, and car on the incomplete M6 and by chartered train to be at this special occasion. The normally busy town centre was empty that Saturday afternoon, as those who had failed to get tickets were at home glued to the television.

Leigh's mascot

As the teams entered the arena the Leigh end exploded with cheering. Leigh were led out by their young mascot, Kevin Ashcroft's son, who had been smuggled into the ground to overcome official disapproval. Instead of the traditional slow concentrated walk to the centre, Leigh players picked out and waved to family and friends in the crowd. One of my friends predicted gloomily, "They are just glad to be here, they think it's enough." He failed to grasp Murphy's psychological battleplan, allowing his players to relieve their tensions and appear to be relaxed. They carried the hopes of all those Leigh fans to motivate and encourage them, plus the incentive of their winning bonus of £100 per man, a low amount even in those days.

As the match kicked off, Leigh slotted straight into their game plan: tight defence, no risks and a strong kicking game. It worked well as Leigh took an early 2-0 lead from a drop goal, the only surprise being the kicker - prop-forward Jim Fiddler.

The tackling on both sides was ferocious and it took all of referee Billy Thompson's vast experience to keep on top of the players. As Leigh broke down the left-hand side of the field through winger, Joe Walsh, Leeds's centre and skipper, Sid Hynes, floored him with a head tackle. On television, Eddie Waring made the prophetic comment: "No man has ever been sent off at Wembley".

Leigh's other potent weapon was their Welsh goal-kicker, Stuart Ferguson. Murphy had felt unable to risk his lack of pace and inexperience in Rugby League at full-back, preferring to play local youngster David Eckersley. Not expecting an open game, Murphy played Ferguson out of the way on the right wing. The Welshman's trusty boot kicked the penalty, ensuring the record of scoring in every round. After 10 minutes, Leigh were now 4-0 up, an encouraging start but still a long way to go.

Leeds at last began to show their footballing skills and mounted a dangerous attack through Holmes and Wainwright. Leigh managed to smother that attack and hit on the counter, but progress was stopped on the fourth tackle and they conceded a scrum in the Leeds '25'. Ashcroft took the ball against the head, Murphy darted away from the scrum and put out a long, flat pass for centre Stan Dorrington to take and score. With the inevitable Ferguson conversion, Leigh led by 9-0. We began to believe it might just happen.

For the remainder of the first half, Leeds looked bewildered as Murphy continued to dominate the game. He dropped a goal himself and opted to trust Ferguson with two long-range penalties on halfway. The first narrowly missed, the second went over to give Leigh 13-0 at half time. The upset was definitely on but surely Leeds would not continue to play so badly.

As expected Leeds came out for the second half in a more determined mood and spent the first 15 minutes pressing the Leigh line. Through a combination of solid defence, Leeds's errors and good fortune, the line held and all Leeds had to show for their efforts was a penalty. No one was firmer in defence than loose forward, Peter Smethurst, who is shown in television close-ups to be grinning hugely as he kept on pulling Leeds players down. Leigh at last managed to get out of their own half and quickly scored yet another drop goal and penalty, so that they were leading 17-2 with only 20 minutes left.

Time was running out for Leeds and their play began to show increasing frustration at their inability to deal with Leigh's and, in particular, Alex Murphy's tactics. This produced the incident for which the 1971 final is notorious.

Exactly what happened is still open to some doubt. Murphy had caught Sid Hynes with a high tackle and the ball moved away. Seconds later Murphy ended up prostrate on the ground. My vantage point high in the stands was too far to see clearly and, in any case, I was following the ball. Television missed the incident, just catching Murphy's fall to earth. There were no alternate television views in those days to check and re-check what happened. Hynes claims Murphy took a dive, while Alex made clear in a recent discussion with me that he had been caught squarely on the chin and that he did not wink at the cameras as he went off, as the popular story goes.

The man that mattered, Billy Thompson, had no doubts, and both skippers left the field at the same time, one on a stretcher, the other disgraced as the first player to be sent for the "early bath" at Wembley. Now we really knew it was all over for Leeds.

Even in his absence, Leigh continued to play Murphy's tactics. Another Leigh attack produced another player who showed he could drop a goal, full-back, David Eckersley. With 10 minutes left, Murphy returned to a hero's welcome and walked slowly to the bench to wild cheering from Leigh fans, and less kind greetings from the Leeds end. The best was yet to come!

With five minutes remaining, Leigh created another opportunity for Eckersley to drop a goal. With the confidence of youth, he took the ball and ran. As he ran towards the end where most Leigh fans were, he seemed to be travelling in slow motion as he dodged and weaved past the tired Leeds defenders, to touch down under the posts. With the inevitable Ferguson conversion, it had now become a rout.

In a final irrelevant twist, Leeds managed a last attack, which the referee adjudged to have been unfairly stopped, and he awarded a penalty try. As the conversion went over the final whistle went (it was whistles, not hooters, in those days!) and Leigh had won 24-7. The unbelievable had really happened, Leigh had not just won, they had crushed the much fancied Leeds team, all due to the genius of Alex Murphy and his ability to get those Leigh lads to play out of their skins. Deservedly he won the Lance Todd Trophy for his individual performance. He managed to overcome his injury to walk up the Wembley steps to receive the Rugby League Challenge Cup.

For Leigh's long-suffering fans the end was climactic. They cheered and cheered as the team paraded around Wembley with the cup held high. Fans were drained, relieved, glad it was over, yet not wanting this feeling ever to go away. Our reluctance to leave the stadium was at odds with our desire to commence the serious celebrations. Inevitably the latter feeling became predominant and we were soon back in central London for the first stage of our commemoration of this historic day.

The larger group of friends began to break up as people went off to party in their own way. The doctor, still dressed in his matchday clothes, came across a traffic accident in Maida Vale and naturally offered his assistance. The policeman supervising took one look at his attire and suggested politely, but firmly, that he move on or he might be arrested.

Together with my companions, after a meal, we ended up in Karl Marx's old drinking haunt, the Museum Tavern, which was full of Leeds fans. In the true spirit of Rugby League, after a little banter, we settled down to a convivial night with the Yorkshire folk, complaining about the terrible southern beer and its even more shocking price.

The following day my brother and I drove back to Leigh to join in the celebrations as the team returned home to receive their heroes' welcome. Everyone was out wearing team colours and streets, shops and even petrol stations were decorated in fine style. My mother, who never went to a rugby match in her life, produced an old sheet on which we just finished painting in red "Well done Lads" as the open top bus carrying the team went past our family home.

We followed to the Town Hall where the square was packed with celebrating fans, greeting the official homecoming. The pub across the street ran out of beer, but no one really minded. There had never been such a celebration in Leigh's history.

Later I just managed to catch the overnight train back to London and went straight into college from the station. I was unshaven, suffering from lack of sleep and a slight hangover and had barely any voice left from all my shouting. I must confess that was not my greatest day as a teacher.

Within a few days, Alex Murphy had left Leigh for Warrington where he was to reprise his trip to Wembley with some of the successful Leigh team. But, later, he returned to Leigh and in the 1981-82 season guided them perhaps even more surprisingly to the League title before another precipitate departure, this time for Wigan.

Although Leigh fans were naturally disappointed when their hero left, but his achievements for the homely small town club were such that we soon forgave him. It was just fantastic to be part of that unforgettable day. For about 10 years any fund-raising event was guaranteed success if it showed the television film of Leigh's big day. And later the video was released by the BBC and fans could watch in the privacy of their own homes.

Rugby League is a sport rooted in its heartlands. This is sometimes regarded as a weakness and does lead to unfair media discrimination. But for those communities it reflects a common hardship, comradeship and an opportunity to forget day-to-day problems. It provides inspiration, entertainment and hope. People experience pleasure at the individual and collective performances that determine matches.

On that glorious day in May 1971, Alex Murphy weaved his magic spells and his team responded to win the Rugby League Challenge Cup. For the town the effect of that achievement was huge, giving the people a huge boost, and is still felt today. For those of us who were privileged to be there, it is still embedded deeply and pleasurably in our memories. When Leigh fans of a certain age get together to discuss the sport, the Wembley win is still a keen talking point. Those too young to be there are excluded from such talk and feel that they missed out on something that may never be repeated.

As long as Leigh remains an epicentre of the game of Rugby League, the feats of Alex Murphy and Leigh's other heroes will never be forgotten.

Post Script

Brian Bowman, the chairman at Leigh when Alex returned and Leigh won the league, told me that by the end of Alex's tenure he was on valium to cope with the pressure. He thought he had signed Murphy on a long-term deal only to read in the press about him going to Wigan. The Wigan chairman, Jack Hilton rang him to see how the ground stood between them. "We will still be mates," said Brian, "come round for a drink." As Hilton left, Brian proffered him the valium tablets saying, "you'll be needing these now." Within a few weeks, Jack rang back to say: "Thanks for the tablets, I need them already!"

Derek Twigg MP: Going back where they belong

The 2000-2001 season is thought by many supporters to have been the most momentous and important in Widnes's history - it was certainly seen as a 'make or break season' It was to be a season that would see a dramatic change in coach, the club's record points win, the club record for the most tries scored in one match by an individual player and of course, the winning of Super League status.

There was deep seated anger and bitterness in the town about the club being excluded from Super League when it was introduced in 1995, many in the game thought it was a shameful decision by those running Rugby League. There was a belief that a lot of jealously existed among some influential people in the game, that a 'small town club' like Widnes had been so successful when so called bigger clubs had been left in Widnes's wake. Other supporters blamed the board for allowing themselves to be out-manoeuvred, while Widnes did not help themselves with a string of terrible results on the pitch.

It is worth noting that the population of Widnes is only 55,000 and yet few clubs could match its success. In the 1970s and 1980s Widnes appeared in no fewer than seven challenge cup finals over a 10-year period, were Premiership winners six times and First Division Champions three times. Then in 1989, in a never-to-be-forgotten match against Brisbane Broncos, Widnes became World Club Champions.

You are left wondering, given the pedigree of the club, why anyone wanting to set up a Super League could leave a club like Widnes out. It did not even make economic sense. Widnes was one of the best supported clubs in the league and was well known for having a large away following. Therefore having Widnes in the Super League meant bigger gates and more money going into the coffers of the other clubs. Their exclusion appears to have been a blatantly flawed attempt to force the game into new areas at the expense of traditional areas where it thrived.

Then to add insult to injury an idea was floated about merging certain clubs and somebody came up with the unbelievable idea of merging Widnes and Warrington! There was outcry in the town. Widnes and Warrington are fierce local rivals. Warrington is a much bigger town than Widnes but could not match the level of support Widnes enjoyed. To merge these two clubs would be a bit like suggesting Liverpool and Manchester United should join forces! 'Big' Jim Mills, then Widnes chairman, had to go onto the centre of the pitch at half-time during one of the matches to categorically deny such a merger would take place.

Widnes were left out in the cold and there was only one way the club - already crippled with debt but still burdened with big contracts - could go: down.

However, among all this gloom and doom there had been a significant development. Tony Chambers had joined the Widnes board of directors when it was formed in 1993 and played a vital role in helping the club make the transition to a limited company. At probably the most crucial point in the club's history, Chambers took over as chairman from the Widnes legend Jim Mills. He inherited a very different club to the one he had fallen in love with all those years ago.

Tony Chambers was born in Coventry and followed Coventry City Football Club. He was introduced to the Chemics and Rugby League by his future father-in-law George Hudson, a life-long Widnes fan and in his own words Chambers "hated it". It took five years to drag him to another match, which was the historic 14-7 defeat of arch-rivals Warrington in the 1975 Challenge Cup Final. "That was one of the most fantastic days I can remember and I was hooked", said Chambers. Over the next 10 years Wembley became the club's second home and Widnes were the undisputed cup kings.

Chambers and his board now began to restructure the club finances, facilities and fan support. They were greatly helped by the decision of Halton Borough Council to purchase the dilapidated Naughton Park. The old stadium and its poor facilities were well past their sell-by date and were totally inadequate for the modem day. A joint venture company was set up to run what is today the new Halton Stadium. Lengthy negotiations took place between the club and the council. A number of applications for lottery funding, stretching over two years were submitted before grants worth £2.59 million were secured and construction work commenced. It was to be another two years before the much-admired Halton Community Stadium was completed.

Halton Council

The role of the local council in helping to turn the fortune of the Vikings around should not be underestimated. Halton Council took a brave decision, against some opposition, to buy the old ground and support the development of the new stadium. There were reservations about the whole deal because of the financial mess the club had got itself into and whether the current board was capable of turning it round. Tony Chambers was a key figure in allaying the concerns that had been expressed.

Thereafter, each season saw some improvement and they had at last, with a new stadium, the platform to showcase their ambition. There were better communications between the board and the supporters with a growing hardcore fan base of more than 2,500. Through the existing supporters club and lottery as well as the new innovations of the Millennium Club, Lady Vikings, and Quid's In group, fans were encouraged to increase their commitment to the cause. Sponsors too were responding positively, but the ultimate objective had yet to be achieved. Chambers and the board knew that when the 2001 Northern Ford Premiership season came around time was beginning to run out.

Super League

There was already talk that Super League bosses wanted to cut the numbers of clubs in the top flight and it was rumoured that promotion would become a thing of the past. This increased the suspicion in the town that certain people were again trying to keep Widnes out of the Super League. Also, just to complicate matters further, the funds from Sky TV for the Northern Ford Premiership clubs were reducing rapidly.

"We also knew that if we really went for it and put all our eggs in one basket, the results could be pretty destructive and we would have to revert to an almost quasi-amateur status. We felt that the team David Hulme had assembled was the right one to achieve the target. At the start of 2001 the board knew this was the most cost effective and opportune time to get promoted," said Chambers. The coach he mentioned, David Hulme, was a popular and much respected former player and Great Britain international, born and bred in Widnes.

Expectations were high and the Vikings got off to a good start with two points against a strong Whitehaven side whom they defeated 22-14. Equally satisfying was the attendance of 3,864. They then went on to gain another good victory by beating Rochdale Hornets on their own ground 24-14. One of the local papers, the *Widnes Weekly News*, commented on the 'large travelling army of fans'. These two wins set things up nicely for the Boxing Day encounter with arch-rivals Leigh. More than 6,500 packed into the Halton stadium for this bruising and hard-fought encounter. The atmosphere was electric with both sets of fans passionate in their support. Widnes were forced to accept second best and in fairness Leigh just deserved to win the match, 25-20.

The next few matches provided a mixed bag of results. There was defeat at Oldham by 20-12; the *Weekly News* commented: "Two holiday defeats in succession have punctured the mood of expectancy that surrounded the Vikings just a couple of weeks ago". Who would have thought at this point that Widnes and Oldham would meet again in the grand final at the end of the season. Widnes then went on to beat Workington and Swinton at the Halton Stadium and drew away at Barrow 6 apiece, although the Vikings went out of the Silk Cut Challenge Cup at the fourth round stage on 11 February, defeated by Bradford Bulls 54-10 at Valley Parade.

York were the next team to visit the Halton Stadium, a day they would want to forget and a day that will be long-remembered by Widnes supporters. York Wasps were on a hiding to nothing before the first kick of the ball, they were so short of players that they had to name two members of the backroom staff on the bench together with coach Lee Crooks who came out of retirement to play. Most of the 2,941 people in the crowd expected a fairly easy routine win for Widnes. As it turned out Widnes notched up a 90-6 victory, a new club record with the popular Phil Cantillon getting a club record try haul of seven.

The match became a giant celebration and Cantillon received a prolonged standing ovation for his record-breaking exploits and Mark Forster got one for recording his 200th career try with a typical touchline hugging run. The Vikings fans also gave Lee Crooks a generous round of applause when he made way after 25-minute spell on the field to help his side. The *Weekly News* paid tribute to him saying "Crooks has been a genuine campaigner for two decades, most of which was spent at the very top and it is a tribute to his love of the game that he was willing to pull on a jersey in such an emergency".

Following a comfortable win, 48-14, against Chorley, the Vikings then lost 26-17 away to Sheffield Eagles and were beaten 18-10 by Doncaster at the Halton Stadium. In his report of the defeat by Doncaster the respected *Weekly News* Rugby League reporter Paul Cook said: "The alarm bells were ringing loudly at the Halton Stadium after a hugely disappointing defeat...". The Vikings left the pitch to a chorus of boos. There was deep unhappiness and dejection in the town about the situation because many felt that the long held dream to get into the Super League had gone.

As the halfway stage of the season approached Widnes were in ninth position and most crucially not even in a play-off spot. "The board was already concerned about the results and discussions had taken place. The pressure was mounting for a change in coach. However we were concerned this might not be a positive thing to do in mid-season and there was no obvious candidate around" said Tony Chambers. But a chance telephone call led Chambers to the right man. David Hulme was sacked after the Doncaster match.

Neil Kelly

The club had interviewed Neil Kelly prior to the appointment of David Hulme but could not agree personal terms and he was keen to gain promotion with his current club Dewsbury. Chambers describes what happened next. "The possibility of Neil becoming coach only arose after he rang the club with regard to some ticket arrangements and I decided to ring him back to discuss other topics. It became apparent in our discussions that things were not happening at Dewsbury in the way Neil wanted and that he might be available. We met in Manchester to discuss the possibilities and personal terms. It was clear from what he said that both he and Widnes needed to change. We quickly agreed a three-year contract. The Board confirmed the contract and, while everyone felt we had missed the boat for the season, it was thought if we could get into the play-offs we could finish the season on a positive note and build from there." The rest is history.

Kelly had a number of reasons for coming to Widnes: "It became obvious that we had come as far as we could at Dewsbury, and though I had learned many valuable lessons and cut my teeth at New Crown Flatt, I was ambitious. The time was right to move on but at that time getting a Super League coaching job was not easy if you were English. So, as Widnes were probably the only club which could be considered certain to get into Super League if they won the Northern Ford Premiership, this was the next best thing to a Super League contract."

But a lifetime in Rugby League meant Kelly was well aware that taking over as Director of Coaching at the Halton Stadium was a big deal. Kelly says "I remember driving home after I had agreed terms with Tony Chambers thinking I am the coach of Widnes! All those boyhood memories of great cup-winning teams and superb players came flooding back. I knew I was taking charge of a sleeping giant in the true sense of the words and I was confident that I could give them the wake-up call they needed,"

Kelly also knew what was needed to turn the club around in the short term. "When I coached Dewsbury against Widnes you always got the impression that they thought they were bigger and better than you and I would use that to gee up my lads" he said. Kelly believes that in the recent past Widnes had gone out and bought a load of players with Super League experience and thought that would be good enough to win the NFP but that meant that "they often played dumb football. I had to change the mentality and change it quickly."

Kelly quickly assessed his playing squad and changes happened immediately, though the new personnel he recruited was not as extensive as some people think. "When I arrived at Widnes I couldn't believe that they didn't seem to know what was their best team and that in vital positions like loose-forward and stand-off they were chopping and changing'. Kelly also thought they lacked a big man up front and a steadying influence at the back. So in came former international full-back Paul Atcheson, languishing in the reserves at St Helens, for a second spell at Widnes. Sean Richardson, a strong-running second-row, also returned to the Vikings having been with Kelly at Dewsbury, and having played in every NFP Grand Final. Big Matty Long and silky skilled Richard Agar followed Kelly from Yorkshire as well and the talented Craig Weston was picked up after Doncaster Dragons ran into financial problems. At the same time Kelly was to get the best out of veterans Tommy Hodgkinson, a rugged loose-forward whose career looked to be petering to an ignominious end, and scrum-half Martin Crompton, who was later to become Kelly's assistant coach.

The board was in no doubt that at the time they appointed Neil Kelly he had the capability but they were all shocked at how quickly things began to pick up.

Against Keighley on 25 March Widnes lost narrowly 22-19 in a spirited performance and there were cheers and applause at the end of the match in stark contrast to the boos of the previous week. In the following match against Hunslet, Widnes coasted to a 64-6 victory in front of 3,253 people. It was clear that the new signings were having an instant impact. The next game against Kelly's old club Dewsbury was a close run thing with the Vikings winning 13-12. The general view after the game was that it was the type of game Widnes would not have won a couple of weeks beforehand.

Then the Vikings lost narrowly 26-22 at Leigh at Easter. But within the club there was a growing feeling that something special might be about to happen. Widnes would not be defeated again that season.

Over 4,000 saw Widnes trail 16-6 against Oldham at half time but in a remarkable turn around they ran out eventual winners scoring 34 points to Oldham's 16. It appeared that Kelly's half-time talk certainly sent Widnes back out in a different frame of mind. A strong second-half performance seemed to be a bit of a trademark of Kelly's Widnes team during the rest of the season. They then went on to beat Hull KR 28-10, Whitehaven 16-14, and notched up a cracking 44-18 defeat of Rochdale. The way Widnes saw off a much-improved Rochdale according to Paul Cook of the *Widnes*

Weekly News "had the hallmarks of a champion side". A crowd well in excess of 4,000 saw Widnes dig deep and fight hard for two points against a battling Featherstone just defeating them 25-22. This was nail biting stuff.

The Vikings then went on to beat Workington 25-6 in front of 1,000 travelling fans in a crowd of 1,761 and hammered Swinton 62-0 at Gigg Lane. There followed more big points victories over Batley 38-15, Chorley 72-18 and York 66-11. They continued their winning ways on 1 July against a poor Hunslet Hawks beating them 42-4 at the South Leeds Stadium. The match was notable for Craig Weston's best kicking display of the season landing seven from seven attempts, in blustery conditions. Just three play-off games now stood between Widnes and Super League.

First came the preliminary semi-final against Rochdale Hornets on 8 July at Widnes. There had been some concern that having had an easy run-in to this match, Widnes might not be at their sharpest. For about an hour of the game there was little between the two sides. The game was poised at 22-20 for Widnes and both sets of players were struggling to keep up the punishing pace. However, the game then turned when the Vikings' Richard Agar put in a 60-yard kick to the corner that got a head and feed at the scrum under the 40-20 rule. The ball went to substitute prop Matt Long who crashed through the tackles to score. Then the excellent Phil Cantillon scored a try from a penalty to secure the 34-24 win for Widnes in front of 4,202 fans. The Vikings now had a fortnight's rest and one game remained between them and the Grand Final.

The Premiership major semi-final on 22 July saw the Vikings up against Leigh - this was as tough as it was going to get. Leigh had easily finished top of the Premiership and had already beaten Widnes twice. Over 2,500 noisy Widnes fans travelled to Leigh to give the team tremendous support. However, after 40 minutes of the match the dream of Super League looked like being shattered, Widnes were on the ropes going in at half-time 12-4 down. But what a turnaround in the second half, the next 40 minutes belonged exclusively to Widnes who got a grip of the game and never let go for the rest of the half.

Nine minutes into the second half the Vikings scored with Damian Munro going over. The pressure told again on Leigh when Percival went over for his second try putting the Vikings in the lead for the first time at 14-12. A further try and a drop goal put Widnes 19-12 ahead. Then there was more drama as Leigh scored a try, which was then converted narrowing the Widnes lead to one point. Widnes came back with Knox kicking a further drop goal followed by a terrific solo try from Chris McKinney. Weston converted the kick and it was all over at 26-18. There were great scenes of jubilation at the end. The *Widnes Weekly News* described the performance as "an awesome display of heart and determination".

Before the game Neil Kelly had sensed that Terzis was worried. "If things had been going right for Leigh Paul would have kept quiet, he said. "There was no point trying to wind us up unless he was trying to put us off our game and there was no way I was going to let that happen'.

Along came 28 July, the Grand Final against Oldham, a beautiful, sunny and warm summer's afternoon. Widnes had sold out of their allocation of tickets and had to send for more, such was the demand in the town. The final was played at Spotland in Rochdale. Long queues of traffic moved at a snail's pace towards the ground passing pubs packed with both sets of supporters, many standing outside in the sunshine. There was a fantastic atmosphere in the stadium with 9,000 fans crammed in, the majority of them from Widnes.

Most Vikings fans felt confident that their team would win and were easily the more vocal of the two sets of supporters. Widnes had a nervous first half, and spurned a number of chances, but led Oldham by 10-4 at half-time. In the second half Widnes looked more confident and in control with man-of-the-match Phil Cantillon touching down 10 minutes after the break. Any remaining doubts about the eventual result were cast aside seven minutes later when Jason Demetriou scored for a second time.

Once Munro, facing his hometown club, had added a further try 11 minutes from time Widnes could afford to relax, despite two late tries from Oldham. Widnes ran out 24-14 winners. At the hooter there were wild celebrations among players and supporters which carried on for some time after the trophy was presented. Super League was now within reach for Widnes.

However, chairman Tony Chambers had other things on his mind in the immediate aftermath of the game - an approach for Kelly from neighbours Warrington needed rebuffing but, with Super League rugby quickly guaranteed, Kelly committed himself to the club for three years.

There had been some uncertainty about promotion and relegation to and from Super League and there was a period of frustration while the powers that be decided what they wanted to do. After a short but tense delay Chambers and Managing Director Tom Fleet made a presentation of Widnes's credentials to an independent panel at the Rugby League headquarters in Leeds. Within hours Widnes's application was granted - the Vikings took Huddersfield's Super League place - and the next chapter in the history of this great club could begin.

Achieving Super League status has had a tremendous impact on the local community. It is true say that interest locally in Rugby League has dwindled over the years Widnes were languishing outside the top flight. Apart from the hard core support many Widnesians would have had difficulty naming more than a couple of the Vikings first team, which was in stark contrast to the star studded teams of the 1970s and 1980s. Local amateur rugby had also suffered with the number of kids showing an interest in the game dropping to an all-time low. It was more common to see youngsters wearing Liverpool, Everton or Manchester United shirts rather than a Vikings top.

However, following entry into Super League the renewed interest in the game and the club has been phenomenal. In the games played so far this season at Halton Stadium most attendances have been in excess of 6,000 and the games against St Helens and Bradford have attracted gates of around 9,000. On Easter Bank Holiday Monday the Vikings played arch rivals Warrington Wolves, beating them in a hard fought contest by 20-14 - this gave Viking fans great pleasure. The match was also noteworthy because it was Warrington's record Super League crowd of more than 9,000. Widnes had at least 4,000 supporters at the game making it more like a home match for the Vikings.

One of the features of the home crowd at Halton Stadium in this first Super League season is the number of children and female supporters that are watching. It is particularly satisfying if walking or driving around the town to see so many youngsters wearing the new Vikings jersey that now seem to outnumber the shirts of leading Premiership football clubs. Such has been the demand for the Vikings home shirt that it was impossible to get hold of one for most April, unless you wanted extra large. They sold out and had to order more from the manufacturer.

Widnes have made an excellent start to their first Super League season - it feels like they always should have been there.

Oldham versus Widnes: Northern Ford Premiership 2001 Grand Final
(Photo: Peter Lush)

Widnes 2001: Northern Ford Premiership Champions
(Photo: Peter Lush)

Derek Wyatt MP: Union and League Merge - Shock: Horror

In 1986 I was asked to write a chapter in the *Shopacheck Rugby League Review*, published by Faber and edited by Tony Pocock, an amazingly loyal supporter of the game. It was an odd invitation for me as I had little or no experience of the game. I'd never played it, and I'd only then been to a single live fixture, at Craven Cottage of all places, to watch Fulham versus Wakefield in 1981. I went principally to watch Keith Smith who as a Rugby Union international had been with me on the England tour to Australia in 1975.

Several England players "went North" in the mid to late 1970s aside from Keith Smith including Nigel French, Ian Ball, Bob Mordell, Adrian Alexander and Mike Lampowski. Nigel was a gifted centre for Wasps and played for England (with me) against America at Twickenham in October 1977. We had both been on the Penguins tour to USSR in the summer to play in the Eastern European Cup against Romania, Czechoslovakia, Poland and the hosts. We had both worked hard on our sprinting and speed off the mark in Tbilisi, Georgia, and we deserved to be selected. Our career paths went in separate directions thereafter. He went to Rugby League and signed for Barrow and though I scored four tries that day at Twickenham, I was dropped for the next match, the opener in the Five Nations tournament and never wore the red rose again.

Ian Ball was ultimately to join French. "Ballie" and I met our Waterloo at Blundellsands in the 1976-7 season. I was then playing for Bedford and we had won what was then called the John Player Cup in 1975 against the favourites Rosslyn Park by 28-12. In the following season we went out to our close neighbours Northampton without a fight, but we returned the next year with our best team and a resolve to win the cup again. We were drawn against Waterloo in the quarter-final and at half time we were 19-11 up.

Five minutes from time we were leading 25-18. Waterloo's recovery was down simply to the mercurial Ball, who reminded me of another player - Tom Brophy - who had also played both codes. Ball had kicked us off the park. I'd had a reasonable game scoring three tries and dropping a goal, but Ball stole the show at the whistle with a remarkable run from a missed touch by our no. 8 David Jackson. He scored under the posts to make it 25-25 and then duly converted. To use a well-known cliché, we were absolutely 1000% gutted. Waterloo went onto the final; we went onto oblivion and Ball found Barrow and Rugby League. I did not know Mordell and Alexander well,

Fulham versus Wakefield Trinity 1981 - Derek Wyatt's first Rugby League match (Photo: Ken Coton)

though I had played against them when they were at Rosslyn Park and Harlequins respectively. However, we played together for London Counties against the incoming tourist teams like Argentina, Australia and New Zealand. In the early part of the 1978-79 season we assembled at Lensbury on a Sunday to prepare for our mid-week game against the All Blacks.

Andy Ripley, a former England and British Lions, led the forwards. Andy was the archetypal player's player. One year, in the 'grey' period between amateurism and full-on professionalism, he received boots from both Mitre and Adidas. Being an absolute gentleman and because he had no wish to upset either sponsor, it was alleged that he wore one Mitre and one Adidas boot while playing for England.

On another occasion when we turned out to an International XV against the Met Police at Old Deer Park to raise money for a police widow whose husband had been shot, Ripley was again the forward leader. For our lineout calls he used the name of Polish Popes since 1650. Not every forward in the dressing room understood the joke (there's only been one Polish Pope since 1650 and that's the present incumbent) but they soon did when Ripley kept calling Pope John Paul at every lineout!

Anyway, that Sunday at Lensbury, Andy chose as the lineout calls, the names of motorways to Oldham (who Mordell signed for). Like the Pope joke, at that time there was only one, the M62. He knew, as a Rosslyn Park player, that the week before Mordell had played as 'A.N.Other' in a Rugby League game and that immediately after All Black game he was going to turn professional.

In the *Shopacheck* chapter, I suggested that if League was to prosper it needed to: twin with clubs in the south, an extension of the brand as it would now be called; offer coaching courses across the UK; concentrate on sport centres not schools and change the way it is perceived on television. I also closed by adding that Rugby League was an infinitely more skillful game than Union.

Interestingly, as an aside, Bob Weighill, then the Secretary of the RFU, reported my article to Dr. Alan Taylor, the Treasurer of the Oxford University RFC. Alan mentioned this to me one day and asked if it bothered me. Given my previous run-ins with the RFU this one joined an ever longer queue.

Stuart Evans

My next association with League came when David Hinchliffe MP asked me to attend a press conference at the House of Commons hosted by the Neath MP Peter Hain for Stuart Evans, the former Neath and Wales prop who went professional with St Helens in September 1987. I had spotted Stuart on another Penguins tour, this time to Brazil in 1984, where I was the coach. Stuart had more natural talent than most of us and had he not bulked up at St Helens he would have had a more successful League career. The point of the press conference was to highlight Stuart's case and his wish to return from a French Rugby Union team (where he was being paid) to Neath. We're talking 1994, a year before the union wall fell down. Stuart felt he could finish his career playing in the Rugby World Cup in South Africa. We were trying to embarrass the International Rugby Football Board (or I. B.) into action.

I had first come into contact with Peter Hain in 1969 when I supported his opposition to the Springbok tour to the UK at St. Luke's College, Exeter. But David Hinchliffe was a first. This led me to being invited to address the All Party Rugby League group on why such a sad old bastard like me had such warmth for League.

David had asked me to talk for 20 minutes and then take questions. The problem was that I couldn't see how I could say much beyond the current hypocrisy in Union - where players had crossed the Rubicon but were in denial - and League, which was straight, community based and a better game. So, I bought with me three mandarin oranges.

I proceeded to juggle the oranges and as I did so I asked the members to reflect on the Murdoch Empire. Each orange was one of his television channels: Star in Hong Kong, Fox in LA and Sky in London. Each orange when juggled was exactly equidistant - eight hours apart. Those lots of eight hours gave him a 24/7 global sports platform that needed millions of hours of sports programming.

Then I said for Star to win new viewers all over Australasia, that League in the UK would have to move to the summer TV schedules so that it matched the Australian League season. While I understood their reservations, the game would die if it didn't move out of the winter soccer slot. I cannot now recall the reaction to this heresy in 1994, but it was barely a year before Super League was launched and the calendar switched to the summer.

It had nothing to do with me, honest gov!

It may seem an unlikely pairing, but I enjoyed David Hinchliffe's company. I think I said to him I was hoping to become an MP but whenever I raised the subject with him he always said I must be mad. I did subsequently win the nomination for the apparently hopeless seat of Sittingbourne and Sheppey for the 1997 General Election where I overturned a 16,600 Tory majority to sneak it by 1,929. I was in the Stranger's Bar shortly afterwards and David came in: "What the hell are you doing here Wyatt?" he asked. "I won my seat" I responded, slightly upset he hadn't followed events. "Lordy lordy" he added. "Is there no end to New Labour?" "There isn't" I jested, "otherwise I wouldn't be here."

Between the mandarin oranges and our meeting in Stranger's, I had helped David with one further issue. He wanted to know how much money was swilling around in the Union game. David was convinced that our players at international, state and / or regional sides and some club XVs were being paid. And he was right. But he wanted proof.

I was able to tell him that at the Customs and Excise office in Bristol they had commissioned the taking of aerial photographs of the senior club sides in Wales. The issue was the Excise expected that there was hundreds of thousands of pounds missing from the clubs' VAT returns. By taking aerial photographs whilst a game was taking place they could then blow up the negatives, do a head count and check the gate receipts proffered by the club against the actual receipts that ought to be paid. Needless to say there was a considerable difference.

There was then a threat of legal action between the Customs and Excise and the Welsh clubs. This was something the Welsh Rugby Union could not let out into the public domain. In fact, they couldn't because of the symbiotic relationship between Glanmor Griffiths, Treasurer of the WRU and Vernon Pugh, another Welshman, as Chairman of the IB.

David Hinchliffe therefore began to ask a number of questions on the Order Paper about the Bristol Customs and Excise project. At first the answers from Stephen Dorrell MP, the First Secretary to the Treasury, were circumspect but eventually Hinchliffe won the day and confirmation came from the Treasury that indeed the Customs people had been taking photographs. QED. Union could no longer hide behind its reducing fig leaf.

Thus in late August 1995 Rugby Union went over. Between 1995 and 2000 the game went through its first phase (adolescence) with fights between the 'old farts' and the wealthy investors at a state or club level.

Understandably, there has also been huge concern amongst the League that its best players like Wendell Sailor and Jason Robinson would be enticed by this system and then transferred to Union without any compensation. There was interest amongst Union to entice League players most notably by Bath but it is only the pace men who will now transfer.

After the 2003 Rugby World Cup in Australia and, if and when, Vernon Pugh ever stands down as Chairman of the IB, I believe the two codes of League and Union would be best served by one administration. I think underneath one world body should be two separate entities:
- the professional game
- the amateur game

I recognise, dear reader, that you might find this a rather shocking proposal. When Super League arrived and Rugby Union became more honest, most pundits predicted one code within five years, but that hasn't happened. I doubt it will. But in the north of England at Leeds and Wigan the idea of both codes with cricket and / or football as partners is beginning to emerge. It's the obvious blueprint for the professional game.

Rugby Union has opened its doors to Rugby League. Murrayfield has been a generous host for the Challenge Cup Final as the game between Wigan and St Helens showed this year. Twickenham seems more ambivalent. The moneymen want the game but a small number of Bufton Tufton committee men are less sure. It's inverted snobbery. Those under 40 (sadly not me) do not recognise these old class barriers.

Rugby League has not been well managed of late and the sports market has probably made it more difficult for it to grow. Its World Cup is a muddle and may not be financially secure. I look forward to 2007 when England (I hope) host the Rugby Union World Cup to there being four simultaneous tournaments - a professional Rugby Union and a professional Rugby League major countries world cup running alongside an amateur Rugby Union and an amateur Rugby League minor countries world cup.

I always was a bit of a dreamer!

The Great Bev
The rugby league career of Brian Bevan
By Robert Gate

Brian Bevan is one of the few rugby league players to rightfully be called a legend. He scored 796 tries in British rugby league, a record that will never be passed. He had remarkable fitness, pace, side-step and try-scoring skill.

The book covers his early days in Australian rugby league, his war-time experiences, joining Warrington and his triumphs there, including the 1950 and 1954 Challenge Cup victories. Also included are his international appearances with the Other Nationalities team, his time with Blackpool at the end of his career, and memories of him from fellow players and supporters.

Lavishly illustrated, the book also has a comprehensive statistical record of Bevan's career. This is the first book on Brian Bevan.

"Brian Bevan: a true match winner and an extraordinary try-scorer"
John Etty – Batley, Oldham, Wakefield Trinity & Yorkshire
"He was an absolute phenomenon"
Colin Hutton – Widnes, Hull & Lancashire
"There will never be as good a winger as Brian Bevan"
Albert Pimblett – Warrington & Great Britain
"He could score tries out of nothing"
Bob Ryan – Warrington & Great Britain

Robert Gate is a pioneering and prolific rugby league historian who spent four years researching and writing this book.

Published in August 2002 at £14.95.

Special offer for readers of this book:
Order from London League Publications for £14.00
(post free in UK, add £3.00 overseas).
Please send your order to:
London League Publications Ltd
PO Box 10441, London E14 0SB
 (Cheques payable to London League Publications Ltd - no credit cards. Sterling cheques only)
ISBN: 190365906X

I, George Nepia
The autobiography of a Rugby legend
By George Nepia and Terry McLean

Foreword by Oma Nepia

George Nepia is arguably New Zealand's greatest ever Rugby Union player. This new edition of his autobiography, first published in 1963, also has new and reprinted material that gives a full picture of Nepia's life and Rugby career.

It has a new chapter by Terry McLean on New Zealand's other great Union full-backs. Other new material includes Huw Richards on the 1924-5 All Black tour, Peter Lush and Robert Gate on Nepia's time in Rugby League with Streatham & Mitcham, Halifax and Manukau, Dave Farrar on his Hawke's Bay Ranfurly Shield career and a review of the 1986 *This is Your Life* programme made 3 months before he died.

The book will be fully illustrated and of interest to followers of both Rugby codes.

Published in September 2002 at £13.95.

Special offer to readers of this book: £13.00 post free in the UK, add £2.00 for overseas.

Order from:
London League Publications Ltd, PO Box 10441, London E14 0SB

(Cheques payable to London League Publications Ltd, no credit cards)

ISBN: 1-903659-07-8

Rugby League Bravehearts
The History of Scottish Rugby League
By Gavin Willacy
Foreword by Alan Tait

Despite never having a professional club, Scotland has a rich Rugby League history. From the sport's earliest years, there have been Scottish players in British Rugby League, including Great Britain internationals such as Dave Valentine, George Fairbairn and Alan Tait.

Since 1995, Scotland have competed on the international stage, including in the 2000 Rugby League World Cup. Since the barriers between Union and League came down in 1995, League in Scotland has developed tremendously, and the amateur, student and development parts of the game are fully covered in Rugby League Bravehearts. The book includes:
- A full record of Scotland's international matches
- Interviews with key Scottish players
- Profiles of Scottish Rugby League professionals
- Scottish players' participation in representative matches
- Scottish Students and amateur Rugby League

Lavishly illustrated, this book will be of interest to all Rugby League supporters and those interested in the development of sport in Scotland.

Published in June 2002

£9.95 net in the United Kingdom.   ISBN: 1903659-05-1

To order the book at a special offer price of £9.00 post free in the UK, (add £2.00 for overseas orders) please write to:
London League Publications Ltd, PO Box 10441, London E14 0SB

(Cheques payable to London League Publications Ltd.
No credit cards. Sterling cheques only)

The Rugby League Grounds Guide

By Peter Lush and Dave Farrar
Foreword by David Hinchliffe M.P.

Travelling to watch your team play away, and visiting new grounds is one of the best experiences in rugby league. Equally enjoyable is going to watch an amateur game or a big match at a ground you have never visited before. This book will help you get to the match and use the ground's facilities when you get there.
The book includes for all the British professional clubs:
- History and description of the ground
- Telephone numbers, websites and email details
- Information on price reductions, catering and facilities for people with disabilities
- Public transport details and road directions, with a local map
- Local tourist information

It also has basic details of:
- The Australian National Rugby League clubs
- French professional clubs
- BARLA National Conference clubs
- Summer Rugby League Conference clubs

Published in April 2001. If ordered by post, includes a 2002 supplement.

Every Rugby League supporter will find this book very useful.

Special offer price for readers of this book: Order your copy for £7.00 post free in UK - add £2.00 for overseas orders (cover price £7.95) from London League Publications Ltd, PO Box 10441, London E14 0SB
(Cheques payable to London League Publications Ltd, no credit cards.
Sterling cheques only)
ISBN: 1-903659-02-7

Our Game
Rugby League Analysis, History & Vision

A national Rugby League magazine published twice a year

Our Game covers the game's history, international reports, current issues, book reviews, 'changing the rules', fiction, obituaries and much more.

Regular contributors include Robert Gate, Tony Collins, Huw Richards, Michael O'Hare, Phil Melling and Craig Wilson.

Subscribe

Four issue subscription: £7.00
Special £10.00 offer:
Three issue subscription plus a copy of **one** of the following books:
- *Tries in the Valleys* - A history of Rugby League in Wales
- *From Fulham to Wembley* - 20 years of Rugby League in London
- *The Fulham Dream* - Rugby League tackles London
- *The Rugby League Grounds Guide*

Back numbers available:
No. 1: Brian Bevan, Central Park, Melbourne Storm;
No. 2: 1954 World Cup, Lebanon, North America, Alex Murphy;
No. 3: 1985 Challenge Cup Final, Cumbria, Andy Gregory,
No. 4: Jim Sullivan, Ashes 1988, Hull FC.
No. 5: Bev Risman on Wembley '68, Yugoslavia, Hawaii and Salford.
£1.50 each or special offer: £5 for all five

- To subscribe, please write to London League Publications Ltd, PO Box 10441, London E14 0SB.
- Please indicate the length of subscription, book chosen if taking the £10 special offer, any back-numbers ordered and your name and address.
- Please indicate which issue you want you subscription to start with.
Cheques payable to London League Publications Ltd, no credit card orders.
To order the current issue, send a cheque for £2.00 to: London League Publications, PO Box 10441, London E14 0SB. (no credit card orders).
Our Game is also available from Sportspages (London & Manchester), Smiths of Wigan, and is on sale at all London Broncos home matches

Sports Books available from London League Publications:

Rugby League:

Knowsley Road - Memories of St Helens RLFC
By Andrew Quirke
Published in August 2001. Features players, coaches and supporters' memories of one of the sport's great clubs
Published at £9.95, special offer £9.00 post free in the UK.

From Fulham to Wembley - 20 years of Rugby League in London
Edited by Dave Farrar and Peter Lush
Published in June 2000 to celebrate the London Broncos' 20th anniversary, the book includes profiles of key players and coaches, supporters' memories, and reports of key matches.
Published at £8.75, special offer £8.00 post free in the UK.

The Fulham Dream - Rugby League tackles London
By Harold Genders
The inside story of how Harold Genders set up Fulham RLFC and won promotion in the club's historic first season. Fully illustrated with full records of that great campaign.
Published in September 2000 at £6.95, special offer £6.00 post free in the UK.,

London books special offer: The two books for £12.00 post free in the UK.

Tries in the Valleys - A History of Rugby League in Wales
Edited by Peter Lush and Dave Farrar. Foreword by Jonathan Davies
Covers the Welsh international team, clubs in Wales and interviews with key people involved in the game in Wales.
Published in 1998 at £14.95, special offer £8.00 post free in the UK,

Cricket:

Buns, Bails and Banter - A Season watching County Cricket
By David Spiller. Foreword by Vince Wells
The author followed Leicestershire home and away in the 2000 season. Captures the unique atmosphere of county cricket today.
Published in 2001 at £8.95, special offer £5.00 post free in the UK.

Order from: London League Publications Ltd, PO Box 10441, London E14 0SB. (Sterling cheques only, payable to London League Publications Ltd, no credit cards.) Add £2.00 per book for overseas orders.

Books available from Robert Gate £5.00 each!!

- *Gone North: Welshmen in Rugby League* (Volume 1)
- *Champions: A Celebration of the Rugby League Championship 1895-1987*
- *The Struggle for the Ashes* (1986)
- *The Struggle for the Ashes II* (1996)

All the above books are profusely illustrated and are available at £5.00 each, which includes postage (United Kingdom only)

****

There Were A Lot More Than That: Odsal 1954

Still available in limited supply £11.95 (including postage, UK only)

****

Gone North: Welshmen in Rugby League (Volume 2)

Hardback edition only, £14.99 including postage. Softback edition is sold out.

To order, send cheques (payable to R.E. Gate) to R. E. Gate, Mount Pleasant Cottage, Ripponden Bank, Ripponden, Sowerby Bridge, Yorkshire HX6 4JL (Tel: 01422-823074)